To M. H. W.

WALTER F. WRIGHT

Art and Substance in George Meredith

A Study in Narrative

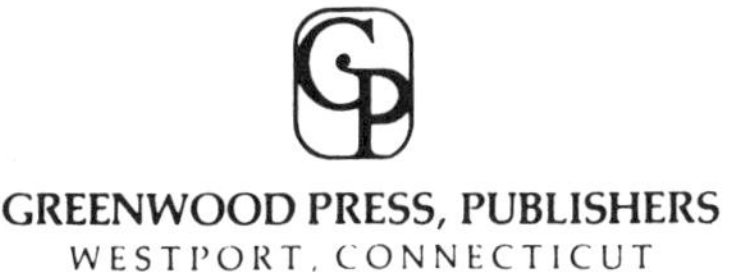

GREENWOOD PRESS, PUBLISHERS
WESTPORT, CONNECTICUT

Library of Congress Cataloging in Publication Data

Wright, Walter Francis, 1912-
Art and substance in George Meredith.

Reprint of the ed. published by University of Nebraska Press, Lincoln.
Bibliography: p.
1. Meredith, George, 1828-1909--Criticism and interpretation. I. Title.
[PR5014.W7 1980] 823'.8 80-14417
ISBN 0-313-22514-1 (lib. bdg.)

All copyrighted quotations from Meredith's works appear with the permission of Charles Scribner's Sons. The quotation from *Wordsworth in the Tropics* is with the permission of Harper and Brothers.

Reprinted in 1980 by Greenwood Press,
a division of Congressional Information Service, Inc.
88 Post Road West, Westport, Connecticut 06881

Printed in the United States of America

10 9 8 7 6 5 4 3 2 1

Introduction

For decades George Meredith has been recognized as a brilliant and yet puzzling writer of poetry and fiction. What I have attempted in the pages which follow is a reinterpretation to clarify both his thought and his art, indeed to interpret the art as the quest for truth, since truth itself became more fully revealed to Meredith as he built his artistic embodiment of it. As the poetry is a vast area in itself, I have considered only those poems which are distinctly narrative in form or immediately pertinent to the study of the novels.

In the first chapter we are concerned with Meredith's basic concepts of life and the literary theory they evoked, in the second with the general characteristics of the world he created in his fiction and the fundamental artistic methods by which he achieved that world. In the remaining eight chapters, grouped in pairs, we approach Meredith's fiction from each of the four major perspectives—the comic, the romantic, the tragic and pathetic, and the tragicomic—which the novelist employed in his search for and representation of truth. Through this approach relationships which are otherwise undiscoverable become recognizable and important. The pursuit of certain truths in *The Shaving of Shagpat,* Meredith's first novel, reappears, for example, in variant forms in his later novels, and the consistency with which he continued the search is remarkable. As Joseph Conrad once remarked, through art the artist attains to the miracle of "creating for himself a world, great or little, in which he can honestly believe." In the light of such a concept artistic perspective and technique become important, for through art an author refines upon his concepts until they become more fully consistent and hence believable.

In romance and comedy Meredith was most at ease. His own enthusiasm and his enjoyment of hidden incongruities enabled him to see life as a romantic and yet comic adventure.

In tragedy he was least comfortable, tending to leave tragic themes undeveloped or to shift to a tragicomic method; yet he sketched the essential lineaments of several tragic characters. It was in tragicomedy that he was most experimental and original, and through it he contributed most to succeeding writers. Though less intense than tragedy, it enabled him to illuminate the recesses of man's mind and his moral being.

Readers who want a full biography of Meredith will enjoy beginning with Mr. Siegfried Sassoon's very readable *Meredith* and the two-volume edition of Meredith's *Letters*. For those who are coming to him for the first time a few guiding biographical facts may be helpful.

Without being autobiography, Meredith's creative work manifests the qualities revealed in his own life. Capable of looking fearlessly at the shortcomings of his age and of his own character, he was nevertheless of a compassionate nature, with warm sympathies and acute emotional sensitivity. He possessed, too, a deep trust in the order of the natural universe and of human life.

Born in 1828, the grandson of a tailor and the son of a merchant for whose personal and commercial attainments he was to have little respect, Meredith appears early to have found in literature the romance not offered by family position. His two years of schooling at Neuwied, 1842-1844, especially prepared him for one of the important influences upon him, that of German literature. The late 1840's and early fifties, when he was starting his literary career, were a very troubled transitional period for the young writer; he seems to have experienced intensely the sense of insecurity and snobbishness which were later to characterize several of his young heroes, most notably Evan Harrington. Also the brittleness of wit of his heroine Diana Warwick accords with the author's own self-assertion at the outset of his career.

The romantic idealization of Mary Nicolls, whom he married in 1849, was succeeded by a clashing of wit and will which Meredith soon afterward paralleled in describing the tragicomic bitterness of his hero in *Modern Love*. After the estrangement in 1858 and even more after his wife's death in 1861, he sought anxiously and with only partial success to gain the affection of their son Arthur, born in 1853. The unhappiness which he endured is revealed obliquely in his letters and is echoed in *The Ordeal of Richard Feverel*. The marriage to Marie Vulliamy, in 1864, began a period of generally happier existence, interrupted by her illness and her death in 1885, but otherwise continued almost until his own death in 1909.

In addition to creative writing Meredith was engaged in other literary activities, the most important being his work from 1860 to 1895 as a reader of manuscripts for Chapman and Hall. Most of his life was lived, in fact, in an atmosphere of books. Long walks varied his routine, and the letters attest, not to a busy social life, but to a deep interest in a considerable number of close friends. There were, especially during the troubled years of his youth, imperfections in his personality which Meredith regretted and at which he laughed with penetrating sharpness through more than one characterization in his novels. But as one reads the whole biography and the poetry and the novels, one feels in the presence of a noble mind.

To Professor Royal Gettmann of the University of Illinois, Professor Edward Wagenknecht of Boston University, and Professors Thomas Raysor and Lowry Wimberly of the University of Nebraska I am deeply indebted for criticism of the manuscript. A summer fellowship granted by the University of Nebraska Research Council facilitated the writing; and Miss Emily Schossberger, University Editor, and Mr. Stanley Moon of the University of Nebraska Press have ably and patiently edited the work and supervised the printing. To A. B. W. I owe an indefinable debt for assistance and encouragement.

Contents

Art and Substance in George Meredith

Chapter One

Philosophic and Literary Tenets

For this the Comic Muse exacts of creatures
Appealing to the fount of tears: that they
Strive never to outleap our human features,
And do Right Reason's ordinance obey,
In peril of the hum to laughter nighest,
But prove they under stress of action's fire
Nobleness, to that test of Reason's highest
She bows: she waves them for the loftier lyre.
(The Two Masks)

A RECENT history of comedy, surveying the range from Aristophanes to the present, loiters for three pages to dismiss Meredith before turning to saltier meat. The novelist is found guilty of complacency because he did not damn his age; and because he wrote little of the lower classes, his art is laid aside as amusement for the few. Meredith would probably have found his critic a lugubrious fellow; and without damning either him or the complacent civilization which too often wants literature to be the housemaid drudge of democratic reform, he would have let the impish comic spirit set up a hum of laughter about his ears. Such laughter would not revolutionize the social order and admittedly it would be heard by few, but it would show the penalty that comes to literary historians as well as to others when they do not "Right Reason's ordinance obey." It would unfortunately find no excuse for waving its victim "for the loftier lyre."

For comedy was for Meredith no servile handmaiden nor yet a beadle with whip or club to scourge sinners self-righteously from the town's end. Though seated a step lower than her tragic sister, the muse of comedy sat enthroned above the hurly-burly and, beckoning the combatants to her feet, whispered to them how to perform less ineptly their own small share in the battle. She did not expect the conflict to cease; she sought only to bring a more clear-headed skill to its waging. It was, in short, the eternal passions which were committed in the heat of the struggle, but in Meredith's belief the cool, dispassionate intellect could alone survey the melee and wisely deploy them or restrain.[1]

When Meredith published *The Ordeal of Richard Feverel,* in 1859, literature was still in the main dominated by what is vaguely termed classical psychology, with its emphasis on the importance of the will. Before his death, as students of the novel are aware, many writers had come to stress the role of the subconscious, to explore the obscure emotional impulses which often shape a man's life unrecognized by his conscious mind. With the new field of exploration there came, too, much experimentation in narrative method. Though Meredith began writing when Dickens and Thackeray were popular, with their traditional straightforward plots and their tendency to hold the individual consciously responsible for his actions, and though he continued into the era of Proust, his literary career does not represent a steady progression from the old to the new. Rather, his early fiction anticipates the new and his late work still has much of the old. In *The Ordeal* appeared subtle illuminations of the subconscious; and *One of Our Conquerors,* published thirty-one years later, differs only in exploring what for Meredith were yet unscanned recesses of the mind. At the same time, he did not waver from his initial appeal to the conscious mind, and he invariably judged man's darkest actions in the daylight that permits conscious choice.

Meredith was also from the beginning given to experiment, trying to bend the narrative form to his wish, whether to include a chapter of lyric prose-poetry or to indulge in a leisurely character or philosophic analysis; in fact, he rarely thought of plot as having a tight dramatic sequence or a uniform epic perspective. Yet he did not use several of the techniques which by 1900 were replacing chronological order with that of psychological awareness, as in Conrad's *Lord Jim*. Though interested in the mental turmoil of his characters, he continued to resort to dots to indicate that a mind had deserted the realm of articulate thought and entered that of the loose association of images—an area which Henry James and others were beginning to open as a rich field for the artist to explore.[2] Some of his most effective scenes are ultratraditional. indeed closely reminiscent of his favorite comic dramatists—Menander, Terence, and Molière—in their brilliant dramatic clash of ideas and types of character; and in such traditional scenes the reader finds both novelty and subtlety. On the other hand, some of his shrewdest character analyses helped in the growth of the psychological novel.

The transitional position of Meredith is amusingly revealed in the history of his reputation among journalistic reviewers and literary critics. His first books were disturbing to conventional reviewers because they did not conform to established patterns. Later, in 1889, William Watson was typical in protesting that the novelist could not construct a narrative; and in the same year Oscar Wilde, a Meredithian enthusiast, wrote in his paradoxical manner the now famous and partially true comment, "As a writer he has mastered everything except language: as a novelist he can do everything, except tell a story: as an artist he is everything, except articulate."[3] As late as

1901 W. C. Brownell, another admirer of Meredith, devoted most of a long essay to complaints against him as a novelist, his major defects being that the world in his novels was too complex to be real and that he diluted passion. Both of Brownell's strictures presumably stemmed from the fact that even in tragedy Meredith seldom moved with classical swiftness and singleness of focus toward a powerful emotional ending. Yet Brownell concluded with a one-paragraph assertion that he was nevertheless a genius. And in his second series of *Shelburne Essays,* in 1905, Paul Elmer More, distressed by Meredith's descriptions of the physical expression of involuntary feelings, protested that there was insufficient stress on spirit, that the conscious will was at times subordinated to the physical body. Clearly each of these writers was perplexed by the newness in Meredith, and More found what he believed were resemblances to the attitude of Zola and the other naturalists, writers to whom the novelist himself seems to have alluded when blaming authors for surrender of the conscious mind. Today, on the contrary, the general narrative patterns of his fiction are safely within the limits of current practice and so present no obvious newness to the casual reader, and his interpretations of life are in danger of being insufficiently appreciated because they have lost not their depth but their novelty. Actually, Meredith was an experimentalist well grounded in tradition.

Not only *An Essay on Comedy and the Uses of the Comic Spirit,* 1877, but incidental allusions in other essays and in the letters reveal that Meredith was a thorough and systematic reader both of literature and of literary theory. A record of his *Belesenheit* could use the scores of references only as samples of his reading. The Greek and Roman classics he studied with commentaries; he knew intimately the major figures of Italian and French literature; and with his early schooling in Germany as a foundation, he was well oriented in German letters, being particularly influenced by Goethe and by the critical writing of Jean Paul Richter. In English literature his knowledge was scholarly and broad, whether in poetry, the drama, or prose fiction.

Like Sir Philip Sidney, Meredith held that literature must unite precept and example. Again and again he wrote, often within a novel itself, that fiction must present ideas; and his Pilgrim's Scrip, Book of Maxims, Philosopher, and other choral commentaries are devices to introduce informal discussion of ideas. Stressing the need of philosophy, he would have all character analysis and all romance philosophic. Poetry, however—and by implication prose fiction—he once wrote, was superior to philosophy by itself in that it wedded ideas and emotions.[4] In short, it presented both ideas and the emotional involvements which arise as soon as the ideas find a home in a human mind. The major province of the novelist, as illustrated in Meredith's own fiction, was the dramatic turmoil within the mind when, having but imperfectly understood the ideas, the mind could not easily resolve apparent conflicts between them or, more often, between the emotions which accompanied them. The resolution of these conflicts for a character or the analysis of the cause of his failure to resolve them made the principal action of a novel. In the most general sense this concept of narrative literature covers many types, whether of Samuel Richardson, Meredith, or Hemingway. Meredith's own place in the history of fiction is expressed in the ideas which he chose to present and the degree to which he regarded them as realities in themselves, on the one hand, and, on the other, the degree to which he recognized the forces that always inhibit and at times even annihilate rational thought.

Underlying Meredith's literary theory are his concepts of the world of nature, of the intellectual and emotional structure of human beings, and of the social order in which the mind can best develop. His own perception of nature allowed him to recognize the ruthlessness in animal and plant struggle for survival; and he considered the life of the savage, that is, the life which adapted itself least from primitive nature, to be uniformly deplorable. Savagery, of course, was not a matter of living in wattled huts; it was a submission to animal standards of culture and, under a veneer of politeness, could dominate an industrial society. To achieve self-discipline man must accept the stern fact that nature destroys the spiritually passive mind:

> Her [nature's] lord, if to her rigid laws he bows;
> Her dust, if with his conscience he plays knave,
> And bids the Passions on the Pleasures browse:—
> (*The Test of Manhood*)

Like the Romantics, Meredith found in nature immediate spiritual inspiration. *Love in the Valley,* the well known Ferdinand and Miranda scene in *The Ordeal of Richard Feverel,* and lines in "Meditation under Stars" typify the exaltation brought by natural scenery; and elsewhere, as in Richard's walk in the German forest, Meredith can speak of the healing and purifying which nature brings. Indeed, in *Modern Love* it is his memory of the swan sailing across the lake that turns the hero's cynical bitterness into tolerant sadness; and in "A Faith on Trial," written upon the fatal illness of the author's wife, it is sight of the cherry tree in blossom which subdues the cry of doubt by suggesting man's kinship with the inherent beauty of the universe:

> . . . natures at interflow
> With all of their past and the now,
> Are chords to the Nature without,
> Orbs to the greater whole:

In such instances it is not the poet's reason which is trying to decide what aspect of nature is good and what is bad; it is his imaginative vision, which verges on enchantment:

A wonder edges the familiar face:
She wears no more that robe of printed hours;
Half strange seems Earth, and sweeter than her flowers.
(*Meditation under Stars*)

An evolutionist, Meredith believed the "Spirit of Life" to be forever unfolding itself within man and nature, with man contributing to the progress.[5] Here in accord with the Positivists, he nevertheless preferred artistic insight to scientific inquiry in identifying man's part in the universal growth. He did not speculate on abstract concepts of ultimate causes, but, both in his poetry and his novels, he was, like George Eliot, preoccupied with the capacities of the human mind. He felt that a man could be held personally responsible for contributing to the spirituality of the universe.

Meredith's favorite trinity, given always in ascending order —blood, brain, spirit—assumes the latent existence of animal joy, reason, and the capacity for aspiring to beauty and goodness:

Each of each in sequent birth,
Blood and brain and spirit, three
(Say the deepest gnomes of Earth)
Join for true felicity.
(*The Woods of Westermain*)

Ideally, blood was not to be suppressed, but, on the contrary, strengthened and at the same time disciplined by brain to contribute to spirit. A vigorous walk through Surrey or a climb in the Alps was good tonic, Meredith believed, whether for himself and his friends, including the famous Sunday Tramps, or for the scholarly young men in his novels; and the forthright assertion of blood as love of man for woman was a fine thing in Richard and Evan Harrington and Matey Weyburn.

Stress on this point is necessary because, though there was ample authority in the tradition of Chaucer, Shakespeare, and Fielding for the frank acceptance of man's animal nature, the novelist believed that his own age in its determination to be civilized was setting up a foolish conflict by repression and under a refined and polished exterior was really perpetuating animality in its rawest form. With the attack by the clergy upon *The Ordeal of Richard Feverel* as an immoral book, he had full justification for reasserting his trinity and for repeating his objections to the artificial education which would build spirit with disregard for nature as expressed in blood.[6]

What then were the characteristics of actual human life that were pertinent to a novelist who sought to be philosophical and to help man find himself in the evolution of the spiritual universe? Man was, first of all, a highly imperfect animal evolving spiritual consciousness uncertainly, with frequent blind straying and stupid blundering, but with a mind capable of instruction through suffering. His course to the extent that he was a being of instinct and physical impulse was often best symbolized by Scylla and Charybdis, which in *Diana of the Crossways* Meredith identified as the "ascetic rocks and the sensual whirlpools." To judge from his novels, those who, like his contemporaries, turned the prows of their ships away from the whirlpools were likely to strike the rocks or perhaps to drown in the pools themselves while drifting astern. Or they might steer a madly fantastic course between the two. The perilous nature of their voyage should always arouse pity and their shipwrecks were of tragic seriousness. At the same time, the zigzag pattern of the course, with sudden reversals of direction, was inherently comic. If they managed to escape complete disaster and keep afloat, the pity would remain. Whether they sank early or after daring sailing, their vagaries had a comic incongruity which in no whit lessened the pity. Some of Meredith's characters, such as Vernon Whitford of *The Egoist,* sail an even course, neither comic nor pathetic, but others, such as Harry Richmond, Sir Willoughby Patterne, Wilfrid Pole, and Diana Warwick, have a precarious voyage; and still others, among them Richard Feverel, the Earl of

Fleetwood, and a number of unhappy women, succumb. Whatever in the form of precept and convincing fictitious example assisted one in charting a path between asceticism and sensuality was for Meredith of philosophic literary value.

Viewed from another perspective, man was psychologically egocentric, prone to resist whatever would disturb his preoccupation with self, yet lonely and incomplete so long as his resistance succeeded. It was a major fault of the sentimentalists of the time that they glossed over egoism as a maladjustment easily overcome. Meredith accepted it as an inevitable condition of human nature. Though he gave no specific illustration, he admitted in the introductory chapter to *The Egoist* that in the youth of a nation the aggressive assertion of the ego could be harmless and might accompany action of benefit to the race. When the ego ceased, however, to exert itself in the mastery of nature and the building of a social order and began instead to resist social change from fear of loss of self-importance, it became defensive and abnormal. Only then should it be castigated and corrected. The instinct would remain, as it was inseparable from the urge to survive; its negative expression as defensive resistance must be destroyed if brain were to develop spirit and evolution were to be a process of spiritual improvement.

Of the seriousness of the perversion of egoism Meredith could find sufficient evidence in literature. Aristophanes and Menander and Terence and Molière had not laughed at man's assertion of power in the growth of a civilization, for such assertion when not morally good was invariably tragic rather than comic. The comic dramatists found much, however, to chastise in those who held defensively to outworn superstitions and who, tacitly assuming that the limits of human attainment had been reached, tenaciously guarded what they thought were their own exclusive domains. In nineteenth-century England itself Meredith could discover almost unlimited evidence of man's fear of change. The resistance to the idea of evolution by those who could not see that it expanded the boundaries of a human mind and saw instead only a shunting of themselves from the center to the periphery was a gigantic defensive assertion of the ego against aggressive new ideas. Though he did not specifically attack anti-evolutionists, Meredith made very clear in his novels that he felt that the clergy were generally among those who resisted philosophic change and who looked upon the soul not as an agent fighting its way upward in a limitless spiritual world, but rather as a precious static entity to be protected from external struggle.

Actually Meredith more directly reprimanded the scientists, including the evolutionists; indeed the reason why he is perenially alive is that he never accepted a significant view or a mode of conduct without looking at once for its possible absurdities and laughing heartily at them. Scientists he found too willing to make science an explanation for everything and so to defend the limited faculty of reason against the encroachment of the poetic imagination. It should at once be pointed out that in neither instance, whether in satirizing the clergy or the scientists, was Meredith passing judgment on religion or on science as they could be understood by the well-rounded philosophical thinker. He was concerned with the popular inertia in religion which retarded change and with a popular inertia no less serious which would make knowledge of scientific fact a protective shell in which the mind of a Sir Willoughby Patterne, for example, could take egoistic refuge against the complexities in the world of the artistic imagination. Putting man in some outer region of the spiritual universe or making him a deterministic creature was contradictory to Meredith's belief in the significance of individual spirituality. At the same time, he believed that the individual mind reached its highest form only when in intimate concord with nature and when self-forgetfully participating in a community of ideas. It was a function of literature to illustrate this truth and to show how affinity of human minds was to be achieved.

In political and social life Meredith found egocentric assumptions almost proportionate to the seriousness of one's convictions. The obstinacy of the political traditionalist is nicely epitomized by Tory Squire Beltham's comment, in *The Adventures of Harry Richmond:* "It's Scripture says we're going from better to worse, and that's Tory doctrine." It is reflected by Everard Romfrey, in *Beauchamp's Career,* by Sir Willoughby, and by the dozen or more others who insist on living in a past age and opposing democratic change. But the radicals, among whom Meredith classed himself, could be equally intolerant and defensive in their determination to twist the world to their views instead of adapting themselves —witness the comic inconsistencies of the radical Beauchamp. Here was a fertile area for literature comic in method but profoundly serious in intent; for as Meredith insisted, we need the mental stimulation provided by society,[7] and yet as soon as we take part in it we lose our detached acceptance of ideals and become the self-conscious defenders of ourselves as the possessors of the ideals. The clash of idea with idea could be examined in a speculative treatise in philosophy, but literature gave the ideas a lively and complex psychological significance by making them struggle for survival in a conflict of instinct and emotion within intricate and humanly inconsistent minds.

Of all the manifestations of egocentricity the relation of the sexes was, Meredith maintained, the most striking and persistent. In novel after novel he gave delightful variations on the theme laid down in *The Egoist* that "the love-season is the carnival of egoism, and it brings the touchstone to our natures." The comic paradox resided in the fact that, though the typical lover, as the novelist saw him, began by worshiping his beloved because she was a goddess, he never thought of following her to Olympus, but at once started plotting to entrap her in his own little windowless hut on the plain. Having glimpsed a new region of crystal atmosphere, he returned defensively to his own dusty haze. And though his divine lady was still to wear her radiant clothing, she was never to be seen withoutdoors lest her satins be smirched and torn; and despite her bringing her own fragrance from Olympus, she was to be humbly grateful for the fumes of devotional incense which obliterated its fragile charm. The pattern of the lover's conquest, identified closely with man's erratic voyaging between the rock of asceticism and the whirlpool of sensuality, was, like it, deeply serious in import yet comic in its incongruous shiftings of course and in the contrast between pretense and reality.

From the egoism of the individual, as Meredith stressed, rose the colossal coral fabric of conventions and mores, built by a multitude of egoists down through history and extended as devotedly by women, the persons who suffered most, as by men. Courtly polish, protective chivalry, the development of a cult of worship of woman might mitigate the crudeness of the act, but they were sometimes actually the devices for the marital rape of her body and the enslavement of her mind. Of crude sexual passion Meredith wrote only briefly and never in detail. Undesirable as such passion might be, it was not likely to be correctible through literature, least of all through literature requiring superior intelligence to comprehend. But the masqueraded form protected by convention might be found in highly intellectual persons, and it was a province of literature to strip away the mask to reveal the crass brutality beneath. At a time when the John Stuart Mills were pointing out the glaring legal injustices to women and later when other advocates of women's rights were demanding specific social changes, Meredith was a steady proponent of revision of the marriage laws, and he once went so far as to approve of trial marriage.[8] Though in his novels he did not propagandize for legal reforms, he repeatedly exposed the actual relation of the sexes to make his readers see that marriage as the possession and control of one mind by another was unpardonable folly. In stressing the mental tyranny involved in the relationship of the sexes, as in each of his other attempts to correct man's egocentric bias, the novelist was concerned with expanding his reader's imagination, an essential, indeed primary, function of the literary artist.

Among authors whose works Meredith praised were Emerson and Montaigne, and he valued them for the completeness of their philosophic views. Of those he admired with strong reservation were Tennyson, Hugo, and his own master, Carlyle. Tennyson he accused of deserting philosophic reality and substituting tunes on sentimental subjects; Hugo he found dynamic in portraying the passions but in need of philosophic discipline; and though a disciple of Carlyle in stripping the clothing of illusion from man, Meredith called him a Titan "heaver of rocks" as distinguished from an Olympian "shaper."[9] Characters in a novel might fumble, and indeed Harry Richmond at the end of his autobiography admits that he is still between a fool and a philosopher; but Meredith expected Harry's story to make the reader achieve an orderly, philosophic sense of values. The life of the passions, that is, of Titans, was the proper brick and mortar of literature, and Meredith's tragicomic characters are all magnificent Titans.[10] But the passions were to be presented in an architectural framework of ideas. The study of the most wayward passions must be part of a contrast of values; the character could roam through a wilderness and end in hell, but his wandering would reveal the nature of the wilderness and show that roads could be built across it.

In a general way Meredith's theory would apply to the works of a diverse group of novelists, including the most objective writers as well as many who have been preoccupied with tracing the vagaries of the subconscious. In actual practice it meant for Meredith strong emphasis on the theme of a novel and a tendency to make his characters symbolize the values which he was contrasting. The conflict within his stories is always of a type that would have pleased Aristotle; the character is at fault, either in having an unsound sense of values or in letting passion destroy his judgment. Though at times the novelist inconsistently turned a scene over to comic eccentrics who contributed little to the progress of his narrative and though he sometimes made obvious, even tedious interpretations of the action which he had objectively presented, the best of his novels have a symmetry based on the weaving throughout of a dominant theme, with variations and with contrasts to heighten its significance.

As one who insisted upon discipline of the emotions Meredith deplored the "rose-pink" of the sentimentalists, and though influenced by *Wilhelm Meister* and *Die Wahlverwandtschaften,* he spoke of the mawkishness of the character Werther.[11] Of sentimentalists he wrote to Maxse in September, 1883, "If I did not take them for subjects of study, they would enrage me past any tolerance." His antipathy in *Diana of the Crossways* and in *One of Our Conquerors* to the other extreme of "dirty drab" or "mal de mer" realism is illuminated by his savage denunciation of Mendès in a letter to Maxse, September 22, 1887, together with his vehement protest there and elsewhere against Zola. He held, somewhat unimaginatively to be sure, that reproduction in fiction of the sordid aspects of life was contradictory to the function of art as a humanizing agent, and that mere realism provided little or nothing that actuality itself did not provide. His own position represented a union of realism and idealism. A devoted reader of Shelley, he insisted that the artist must bring to actuality an idealism which permitted him to perceive and to exhibit the reality beneath the chaos of the external. His dictum in a letter to Jessopp, September 20, 1862, typifies the romantic perspective in literature:

> Between realism and idealism, there is no natural conflict. This completes that. Realism is the basis of good composition: it implies study, observation, artistic power.

> . . . A great genius must necessarily employ ideal means, for a vast conception cannot be placed bodily before the eye, and remains to be suggested. Idealism is an atmosphere whose effects of grandeur are wrought out through a series of illusions that are illusions to the sense within us only when divorced from the groundwork of the Real. Need there be exclusion, the one of the other? The artist is incomplete who does this. Men to whom I bow my head (Shakespeare, Göthe; and in their way Molière, Cervantes) are Realists *au fond.* But they have the broad arms of Idealism at command. They give us Earth; but it is Earth with an atmosphere." [12]

Meredith himself sought to keep in close touch with actuality to the extent of sometimes using actual persons and incidents in his stories. But he interpreted them in reference to what he understood of psychological principles, and he chose them initially because he believed that they exemplified themes. When successful, as in *The Tragic Comedians,* he gave to the actual historical persons motives for their actions where the memoirs were scant and ambiguous. When he fumbled in *Diana of the Crossways,* it turned out that the historical incident which he believed had occurred—the betrayal of a state secret—had actually not taken place, but the weakness of the novel was in the author's inability to bring to his own incident the motivation to make it plausible. Realism, as interpreted in his letter, is what gives verisimilitude to his scenes, as in the excellent sketches of London; and it is sometimes the lack of it that leaves his minor characters uninteresting abstractions. But it is idealism which makes his best-drawn characters symbolize truths. When tracing the shoddy parasitism of Algernon Blancove in *Rhoda Fleming,* Meredith supplied extensive realistic details on his gambling and his hand-to-mouth struggle to survive, but he had first of all in his mind the ideal concept of a man with the survival-of-the-fittest amorality of the beast. The external phenomena were subordinate to the novelist's use of Algernon in the interpretation of his theme.

Though he wrote little about his methods of composition, a letter to Baker, July 22, 1887, reveals his emphasis on character and scene—with no mention of articulation of plot—and his defense of his highly intricate style of expression:

> My method has been to prepare my readers for a crucial exhibition of the personae, and then to give the scene in the fullest of their blood and brain under stress of a fiery situation.
>
> Concerning style, thought is tough, and dealing with thought produces toughness . . .
>
> In the Comedies and here and there where a concentrated presentment is in design, you will find a 'pitch' considerably above our common human; and purposely, for only in such a manner could so much be shown. Those high notes and condensings are abandoned when the strong human call is heard—I beg you to understand merely that such was my intention.

Clearly the novelist considered his fiction to be at its best a thoughtful, indeed philosophic, distillation of life and at the same time a conscious work of art fusing idealism and romance in its tone and pattern.

Humanly inconsistent, Meredith often fell short of his own ideals of composition. Blaming Hugo for working too much with black and white characters, he made his own Vernon Whitford, Redworth, and Matey Weyburn paragons of good sense, learning, and virtue. Protesting, too, in *Sandra Belloni* that readers wanted to read about puppets and that he would at least put noses on those he gave them, he could still imitate Dickens' eccentrics, sometimes with only one distinguishing feature; and he never freed himself from Dame Quickly and Juliet's nurse, or from the stock clowns of ancient as well as English comedy, but continued to depict loquacious servants who spoke with erratic idiom and rambled around the point, yet were likely to slip into their digression a phrase of profound shrewdness. Despite the shortcomings, however, in such unrealistic sketches—the novelist himself trimmed away some in revision—his novels at their best approach his ideals. It is when his dramatic representation of complex motives begins that idealism and realism work together to create not only noses but subtle indentations in the folds of the brain. It is then that comedy, by laying bare feelings and ideas, performs its function of stripping romance of tinseled illusion and tragedy of the taint of unreflecting sentimentality. Then the world in which the characters and we, the readers, move is revealed to be not an artificial realm, with its dinner parties, *fêtes champêtres,* and witty conversation, but the composite of a multitude of human minds, each a veritable world within itself, yet each possessing spiritual affinities with others to make broad symmetric patterns and reveal general truths.

Chapter Two

The Tenets Enclothed: The World in Which the Characters Move

Our world believes it stabler if the soft
Are whipped to show the face repentance wears.
Then hear it, in a moan of atheist gloom,
Deplore the weedy growth of hypocrites;
Count Nature devilish, and accept for doom
The chasm between our passions and our wits!
(The Sage Enamoured)

If no literature existed to influence him, a writer might presumably observe the world around him, generalize about it, and create fictitious illustrations to express his conclusions. In actuality, of course, the novelist comes to his task with a background of reading and a concept of his art form, and it is not easy to separate observation from reading as a source of his conclusions. The process of invention which fiction requires further complicates the relationship. An author may develop a fondness for a particular kind of traditional literary character and then create a special set of conditions in which to portray his own version of the character. Such a milieu, while having verisimilitude as a sketch of the author's own time, may be atypical of the age as a whole.

When we speak of the world in which Meredith most often placed his characters, we cannot say absolutely, "This is Victorian England." Rather, we must add, "as it was seen by a man of extensive literary learning and of very pronounced convictions about man's sensual-ascetic nature, his egoism, and his proneness, from lack of wisdom, to inflict sorrow." Detailed analysis has been made of Meredith's debt to Peacock,[13] and if anyone wishes at all to demur, it can be only to say that other authors could also have supplied some of the same motifs. More casual notation has been made of his indebtedness to such diverse writers as Ariosto, Shakespeare, Richter, Goethe, and Herbert Spencer, to name a few; and a reader finds incidental resemblances to the works of almost any previous comic dramatist of stature. One is consequently aware that Meredith was very much a product of literary history, that he reflected in his own writing the motifs and situations which he liked in his reading. But there is in his borrowings a basis of selection; and since his themes are concerned with what we know, by reading his contemporaries, were current issues and attitudes, it would appear that his convictions themselves were as much based on his study of his own time as they were preconceptions with which he approached it.

Meredith was not interested in giving a panoramic sketch of all the social ranks of Victorian England. We need not suppose that he was indifferent to everything of which he did not write, for such an indictment would bear hard on any author. But he accepted as his province the aristocracy and the upper-middle class because he found in them an ample range; and only rarely, as in parts of *Rhoda Fleming,* did he try a different scene. It was not that a laborer's wife would have a less poignant sorrow than Lucy Feverel nor that a frequenter of pubs would undergo a less tragicomic suffering than the famous Alvan; but Meredith was concerned with those ills in society which comedy might correct by laughter because they were the result of artificial civilization and with those tragic ills which, when found in persons of prestige and power, wrought harm not alone to the protagonist and his family but eventually to the multitude. Moreover, despite his comic exposure of snobbery and of the foolish vulgarity that could accompany rank and wealth, Meredith followed Goethe, Jane Austen, and a good many others in believing that leisure to read books and freedom from the burden of hard physical toil could increase, not virtue, but subtlety of personality. As he indicated in his *Essay on Comedy and the Uses of the Comic Spirit,* he was writing for the cultivated reader; and though he deplored the limitations of English culture, he expected to find his readers mainly in the leisure classes. His comedy would therefore be most pertinent if directed at the veiled shortcomings of his audience. Actually he was more generally popular in America than in England, and it is difficult to imagine some of his own upper-class characters reading his books. As to his tragic scenes, it is likely that in writing mainly of upper society he was also influenced by a tradition that went back to Aeschylus.

As a novelist Meredith did not need to concern himself with all aspects of the subjects with which he dealt. We know that there were forward-looking statesmen in Victorian England, that many clergymen were religious and intellectual, that a woman might live her life without being legally persecuted by a selfish husband—in short, that the common heritage of intellect and generosity did not miss a century. In fact, only in a civilization which was in the main decent could Meredith's most admirable characters obtain an audience. But as a writer, whether comic or tragic in aim, the novelist was preoccupied with the ways in which, despite its general excellence, civilization went astray. In the incongruities that resulted from its erring was substance for pity and often for corrective comedy.

It was a major complaint of Mill in *The Subjection of Women,* 1869, that the British accepted social conditions with the assumption that what had persisted must be good. Meredith probably read Mill's essay, and he certainly agreed with its protest. He believed that the actual economic order and the social habits related to it were disordered accretions and that outworn beliefs and modes of conduct were not only preserved but, as in the Jocelyn, Romfrey, and Patterne households, enveloped in a nebulous aura of sentiment. Even those conditions on which English economic survival depended were likely, he felt, to be accepted dishonestly; one reaped the profits of trade while despising their source. Thus, young Rose Jocelyn speaks admiringly of ships, but scornfully of the trade which floats them. She is not very blameworthy, as she knows no better, but she naïvely reflects the prejudices among which she has been reared. Nineteenth-century English aristocracy, as Meredith saw it, tended to be feudal in sentiment, lethargic or resistant to political reform, and as feudal as possible in economic practices. Rich land and mine owners, such as Sir Willoughby and Fleetwood, set themselves up as medieval barons although the function of a baronage had been lost. The upper classes held fast to their heritage, with its patronage and its freedom to be idle, but their clinging was a negative, defensive thing.

One recalls that Romans who had begun their careers in shops and achieved riches would sometimes change their names and become country gentlemen. The distress which British investors, sometimes including the nobility, experienced at thought of their being tainted by trade was, in short, no limited Victorian phenomenon; but in Meredith's view it was none the less the abettor of far-reaching hypocrisy. In foreign affairs the hypocrisy expressed itself as exploitive imperialism disguised as humanitarianism. Even so kindly a man as Everard Romfrey, who condemns Manchester manufacturers for overworking children, can speak of Negroes as a commodity, a source of labor; and it is assumed by him and his friends that the British laborer when not kept under feudal patronage is the natural opponent of his employer, trying to take from him the profits which he must have to preserve the culture of England.

Except for that strange episode in the 1860's when as a contributor to the *Ipswich Journal,* he sometimes wrote to please his conservative publisher,[14] Meredith was what he chose to term a radical. But he did not expect any sudden reversal of attitudes by either the landowners or the owners of mercantile enterprises. He declined to construct a paragon of day laborers for contrast with the idle Lord Fleetwood, and his most virtuous poor accept a feudal relationship with their economic masters. What he took for study was the working of minds which held fast to rank and wealth but gained no security therefrom and, in their unrest, caused others as well to suffer. A Squire Beltham, despite his unimaginative bluntness, is an honest feudal lord, and his tenants like him. An Everard Romfrey, on the other hand, badly jolted in his *amour-propre,* is eager to take as devotion to himself the humble tribute which the poor involuntarily pay to his newly inherited earldom. And a Sir Willoughby loftily commits the most exquisite tyrannical cruelty while glamorizing himself as a benevolent fairy-tale prince.

Of the crass economic understratum of Victorian custom, marriage traditions were for Meredith among the most serious evidence. What should properly be a communion of two imaginative minds in quest of mutual inspiration was often an uncouth compromise between desire for money and concern for social rank. Marriage for money is so commonplace in the world of Meredith's novels that young Harry Richmond, accepting, as Rose does, the sentiment of his time, can approve his father's attempt to marry a naïve woman merely to secure her wealth. Though the evil of materialistic alliances is most tragically revealed in the French system, which wrecks the happiness of Renée, other loveless marriages in *Beauchamp's Career* and in such novels as *The Ordeal of Richard Feverel, One of Our Conquerors,* and *Celt and Saxon* are the bitter results of concern for feudal rank and for money. The fate of portionless girls is always pathetic; Chillon, for example, speaks frankly of his sister's disadvantage from lack of a dowry.

In a marriage which must preserve feudal traditions, where wealth was inherited, not earned, the stultification of intellect was serious for the husband, and it was deadly for the wife. Men did not often do useful work, but they could occupy themselves with management of their estates and they might enter parliament or pursue some gentlemanly profession. Women, denied a profession, were without exception bound to a life of idleness or to such substitute activities as could in no way express their talents. Even the management of a woman's own money was considered the proper business of a man unless she were an Amazonian independent. Thus, Colonel Halkett must supply Cecilia with a husband because only a man, he assumes, can look after her wealth; she has been trained for a "beautiful servicelessness," to quote Beauchamp's thoughts.

The unimaginative calculation which fostered the combining of incomes or family prestige was timidly concealed, Meredith felt, by a faint haze of sentiment. When Dacier and Constance Asper marry, society, the novelist tells us, is "oriental" in magnifying the holiness of the occasion, which, he implies, makes Constance a member of Dacier's oriental harem, no less a harem for having but one tenant. Yet society is only glorifying the climax of a pattern designed by the two families, who, despite the temporary wayward independence of Dacier, have brought pressure for the marriage as relentlessly as if the two had been betrothed at birth.

Meredith did not ignore the importance of money for persons accustomed to a prosperous standard of culture. He would not ask that all women have the courage of Aminta to cast aside necklaces and bracelets and join a poor schoolmaster in a perilous adventure. Thoroughly disillusioned as to any systems which would change man's circumstances from without, he was yet hopeful of effecting gradual changes from within. He would have an owner of an estate match his prerogatives with a sense of responsibility, and he would have worldly concerns in marriage subordinate to intellectual friendship and romance.

Of nineteenth-century social life in the narrow sense of the term, that is, the cultural and recreational activity of the upper classes, Meredith gives extensive portraits. In sketching the conduct of true ladies and gentlemen he is often as careful as Jane Austen to call attention to its excellence, and his elegantly polite characters remind one of the principals in *Die Wahlverwandtschaften.* In drawing the uncouthness, whimsicality, and comic incongruities, on the other hand, he reminds one of a tradition which includes Shakespeare, Fielding, Dickens, Peacock, and Molière.

Believing that the Englishman was often a dull fellow when left to provide his own entertainment, that he was self-conscious in drawing-room conversation with women, that he had little taste in art, music, or literature, Meredith exposed the pretense with which he disguised his lack of urbanity. Though the novelist himself could become enthusiastic about the flavor of good wine, his men sometimes linger at the dinner table merely because they are at a loss when they join the ladies. In *Beauchamp's Career,* Warder-Devereux is so little able to discuss ideas with women that he makes a refuge of his pipe, and when he dies his wife is "the widow of tobacco ash." The Duchess of Dewlap once remarks, "It is so funny to be having a duke instead of a husband." And trying hard to find anything commendable in the dissipated Edbury, Janet Ilchester must be contented with the fact that, like herself, he enjoys sports. Though scholarly and professional work does get done and some of the better characters are barristers or scholars, Meredith's gentleman is ordinarily trained for no useful occupation. He may take a turn in politics, but without special background, and he is not a well-read man. Following an animal cycle in the sating of his instincts, he is often, in middle age, the victim of his earlier physical appetite; instead of pruning them away, he has usually intensified the excesses in whim and mood which characterized his trial-and-error youth and has now become a crotchety, dyspeptic boor. At best he may be a dilettante, patronizing scholars or poets and dabbling in science. At worst he is a parasite in the Roman sense of the term, spinning out a bored existence that may even end in suicide. He has lost the earlier English spirit of fun and, except for fox hunting, gets little athletic excitement. But, above all, he refuses to exert himself to achieve an interesting personality. For Meredith, on the contrary, a cultivated man was one prepared to take his part in a social orchestra; the metaphor was indeed a favorite of the novelist to characterize an ideal meeting of minds of the two sexes.

The education of women and their position in social life made for Meredith a pathetic paradox. Latin, as Aunt Bel pointedly mentions in *Evan Harrington,* was an obstacle to marriage; the gentleman, we are to suppose, might well fear that a woman of leisure could maintain an interest in Latin and other learned subjects that would remind him of his schoolboy inadequacy. A woman must be cautious in speaking of politics; she should limit her remarks to personalities, as it would be awkward for a Melville Jocelyn to stammer out his ignorance of statecraft in a serious discourse with a woman. She could botanize, and Meredith finds some charm in the botanic interests of Selina in *Lord Ormont and His Aminta,* but then she would be in the elegant tradition of an Ann Radcliffe heroine, as her interest must be aesthetic, never really scientific. She might learn music and she would have some chance of being encouraged to achieve exceptional skill, but a Sandra Belloni must still submit to being patronized by the musically untutored Poles. Other accomplishments she might have, and these, along with music, were directed toward making her vivacious in a drawing room. Unlike the average man she was expected to catch the mood of others and to draw them out. Even the gentle, retiring Laetitia Dale succeeds in making Willoughby a much more lively-minded man than he would be without her. But when a Diana Warwick lets her wit and her knowledge of art and politics become apparent instead of submerging them beneath a soft exterior, she is at once a fair mark for censure, both by the men who can not match her and by the women who have hypocritically acquiesced in the subordinate social role of women.

Riding well was a merit accepted by Meredith's gentlemen as much as by the author himself, but it did not include anything strenuous. Rose Jocelyn, it is implied, is more daring on horseback than most girls, and yet she must drop to the role of inciting Evan and Laxley to risk their necks in a race. Janet Ilchester rides well and is pleased that Ottilia does too, but Janet, like Rose, is a Meredithian heroine in her atypical courage, and Ottilia's riding is only grace on horseback. Carinthia's agility in the mountains, Clara's footracing with Crossjay, and that amazing feat of swimming on the part of Aminta—these are all what Meredith thought should be, and for each of them there are contrasting pictures of the harem existence of others.

In the first version of *The Ordeal of Richard Feverel,* Carola Grandison, still a young girl, openly wishes she were a boy; and the bitterness in the lives of Margaret Lovell, of Livia, Countess of Fleetwood, and of Mrs. Mountfalcon is in the helpless negativeness to which their sex commits them. In *Celt and Saxon,* the women who have started a laundry are again Meredithian examples of extraordinary courage, yet even they are in the business as a charity, so that, though eccentric, they have not lost caste. Without acknowledged serious occupation women of spirit are in the anomalous and nerve-destroying position of studying to suppress or disguise their natural wish for bold self-expression. They are in danger of becoming self-conscious and sentimental in the constant war between their desire for fulfillment of their natures and the necessity of denying that desire.

With no chivalrous adoration of women a Lord Ormont, spokesman, Meredith implies, for a large number of his compatriots, can insist on the separate education of boys and girls so that the girls may possess a seductive strangeness when the love season sets in. By no means alone in his urging coeducation, Meredith was among those who found enticement to vice the consequence of a young man's lack of acquaintance with girls, and loneliness or even brutal horror the fate of girls reared in segregation and then suddenly thrust into a situation foreign to their training. To contrast with actual conditions, Meredith depicted men's and women's search for that naturalness which convention had thwarted. His love stories include the cautious approach of two minds—a Diana and Redworth, Clara and Vernon, or Aminta and Weyburn—each using the other as the touchstone to test his own worthiness. The proper relationship of the sexes was not an obliteration of difference of interest. The heroines are best when thoroughly feminine and purified of the wish to imitate a masculine role; the men are freest and most masculine when they do not think of women as their intellectual satellites.

The moral standards which the novelist ridiculed were at times related to general Victorian economic and social life, but more often specifically to the conflict of the sexes. Possession of love without obligation is the masculine ideal, whether of Sir Willoughby or Sir Austin Feverel, both of whom cloak their wishes under sentiment, of Lord Ormont, who pretends that seduction of affection is the legitimate end of a fair contest, of Heriot, who is crassly indifferent to the fate of girls whom he has seduced, or of the country-bumpkin aristocrat, Harry Jocelyn, who acts from mere irresponsible instinct. In the story of Diana Warwick, in *Beauchamp's Career,* in *One of Our Conquerors,* indeed in almost every novel, Meredith repeated allusions to the chase; a woman was fair prey, first to be hunted by the lawless, and then, if captured, to have her reputation devoured by the moral hypocrites, male and female. One by-product of civilization was its development of sentimentalists, and one aspect of sentimentalism was hypocrisy. The novelist wrote of the narrowness of collective woman, ready to pounce on unconventionality, and particularly of the humbug of the middle class, for whom conventionality was as much social as moral insurance. Woman was to be a strong "fortress"; yet since fortresses are passive, she must paradoxically be helpless and so in need of man's protection.[15] She was to give dignity to man's life, yet live a harem existence. And she was expected to provide man with an alluring chase and then to suffer punishment for her charms when he chose as mate not the exciting object of the hunt but a gentle candle-worshiper, such as Constance Asper. The ludicrousness involved in expecting two utterly different things of woman and then condemning individuals was one expression of polished barbarism, most pointedly asserted in *The Tragic Comedians,* but illustrated many times.

Hypocrisy, as the novelist saw it, did not stop with pretense at ethics, but often wore a halo of religion. Besides attacking Puritan injustice and the prudish Puritan restraints on literature—restrictions which would hamper the natural denouement of a novel—Meredith deplored what he termed the "cant" of such a phrase as "Christian gentleman."[16] Essentially such cant was a mask for intellectual lethargy and moral cowardice, which would use sweet words to arouse sentiment and evade grappling with actual ills. Though he counted the Reverend Augustus Jessopp among his friends and intrusted Arthur's education to him, Meredith wrote in January, 1870, to Maxse:

> The Parsonry are irritating me fearfully, but a non-celibate clergy are a terrific power. They are interwound with the whole of the Middle class like the poisonous ivy. Oh! for independence, that I might write my mind of these sappers of our strength.

In his novels there are no portraits of really admirable professional churchmen. For the most part his clergymen enjoy idleness. They are conservative and dependent on preservation of patronage; they may sycophantly seek advancement, even aspiring to marry the daughter in the household where they tutor or give spiritual comfort. Barmby, though doing some kind of social work, is personally repellant to Nesta, and the curate-tutor of Harry Richmond is a fool. Barmby attempts eloquence about a French cathedral, but neither he nor the others ever achieve exaltation of spirit. They sometimes thrive because they offer melancholy solace to sentimental women; or, as in the example of the Jesuit Lord Feltre, they invite a moral coward, Fleetwood, to evade honest retribution for his sins. In contrast, the fairy-tale captain in *The Adventures of Harry Richmond* is a practising Christian, and the equally unorthodox artisan-preacher, Mr. Woodseer, in *The Amazing Marriage,* leads a life of Christian charity.

An admirer of Molière need get no special credit for variation on the theme of Tartuffe. Hypocrisy had long been an established subject for a writer's invention. But although we cannot absolutely judge the moral and religious tenor of our own day and still less can say that this or that interpretation is an accurate evaluation of the past, there is evidence that Meredith's views were held by contemporaries who had ample experience from which to develop impressions. Among the fruitful sources of information, for example, on the nineteenth-century curate are the text and footnotes in the Shakespeare Head edition of the Brontë letters, and a comparison suggests that Meredith's clergymen are restrained portraits of faults which existed in broad, almost caricatural outlines in actual men. Meredith would seem to be at the same time indebted to a literary heritage and interpretive of contemporary life as he saw it.

Though he could write of our seeing the comic faults of one we love without loving him less, the novelist demanded a fearless reckoning of those faults in the loved one; and though he would also agree that we can value civilization, he would expose the illusion that there was no barbaric warfare present. It was in a world of inherent conflicts exaggerated by every attempt to ignore them that life must be lived. It was such a world that Meredith created for his characters, and his art is revealed in the manner in which they work out their destinies in it.

The world of a Meredithian novel, even when, as in *The Adventures of Harry Richmond,* the author traces the coming of age of the hero, or when, as in *Vittoria,* he seeks to interpret a historical situation, is not a tightly woven narrative, but rather a series of dramatic scenes, with often little or no articulation from scene to scene. The purpose of each stage-like presentation of the characters is the exhibition of a protagonist's values in juxtaposition to contrasting ones. A character is not developed in reference to a multitude of realistic environmental details. But in the world which Meredith creates there come and go a great number of characters—in *Vittoria* E. J. Bailey has counted one-hundred and nine, in *Harry Richmond* one-hundred and sixty-nine—who are introduced, often for a brief incident, to typify an idea or an emotion with which the hero must be concerned. He moves, consequently, not so much in a photographically reproduced scene, even when, as in *Vittoria,* an entire civilization is drawn upon for materials, as in a world of abstracted values, where the follies and virtues of an age are personified by characters who sometimes have no existence for the reader apart from the moment they are on the stage. The psychological changes of a hero are presented mainly in terms of his actions as he moves from one scene to a very different one and later perhaps again to one closely resembling the first. Though a novel sketches enough of the total milieu to provide a setting for the action, the protagonist is placed in a foreground of ideas, where his own values are revealed by direct contrast with those of others.

The scenes are often so balanced that we see the characters grouped as on a Watteau canvas. For a moment two of them speak in the foreground, but the small groups beyond soon come up to join them and thus to remind us of the complexity of their world—witness the many dinner and drawing room scenes, the pageant effects in *Evan Harrington,* the musical evenings in *Sandra Belloni* and *One of Our Conquerors.* In each of these the principal persons are briefly detached from the main social orchestra, even as soloists are in a musical one, but they blend with it again and are best understood in relation to it. When Meredith speaks in *Rhoda Fleming* of social gatherings as ideally orchestral and when in *Beauchamp's Career* he draws the contrast between the self-sufficiency of the organ and the skillful coordination of the orchestra, he is really commenting on the presentation of life in his own novels.

The shift from one scene to another is frequently not so much for logical narrative progress as it is for showing in apparently diverse worlds a variation of a common theme or, again, for emphasizing a contrast of two worlds dominated by conflicting spiritual perspectives. The gipsy life of Kiomi is as of another universe from the court existence of Ottilia; the natural simplicity and love of home in the first picture of Carinthia is ethereal contrast to that of the gambling-resort ennui and baseness which follows. It is not that Meredith was different from other good authors in consciously planning these contrasts. The point is that he worked usually in terms of dramatic scenes and that the progress of his story, both as a portrayal of his age and as the psychological analysis of his characters, must be measured by setting each scene as a whole in juxtaposition to those that have gone before.

Whatever the arrangement of the parts, the theme emphasized or the principle underlying the action of a Meredithian novel is that modern civilization, the world in which the characters live, is both tragic and comic in so far as it is built in contradiction to nature. The romantic childlike wonder and simple life of Crossjay are good; the cautious preoccupation with man-made distinctions, as shown in Sir Willoughby, is comic, and the denial of nature by Sir Austin Feverel is tragically evil. Nature itself is a primary force, whether influencing character through its physical landscape and climate or symbolizing a norm of action that allows wholesome exercise of blood and imagination. It is the ultimate struggle of character with this force that gives the dramatic tension in a novel. The world created by Meredith is thus a symbolic representation in which the characteristic features of one age are used in the expression of universal artistic values.

Chapter Three

Discipline by the Comic Spirit

O lived the Master now to paint us Man,
That little twist of brain would ring a chime
Of whence it came and what it caused, to start
Thunders of laughter, clearing air and heart.
(The Spirit of Shakespeare)

THE COMIC characters in Meredith's fiction illustrate Aristotle's dictum in that they are of a lower order than tragic ones: they have not been waved "for the loftier lyre." With only a slight alteration in perspective some of them would be revealed to be tragicomic, and indeed we do pity them for their folly and also suspect that we are more like them than we dare admit. But both our pity and fear are, under the author's rigorous discipline, firmly subordinate to the critical intellect.

Of what we may call simple comedy Meredith listed the functions in his *Essay on Comedy and the Uses of the Comic Spirit,* 1877:

> Men's future upon earth does not attract it; their honesty and shapeliness in the present does; and whenever they wax out of proportion, overblown, affected, pretentious,

> bombastical, hypocritical, pedantic, fantastically delicate; whenever it sees them self-deceived or hoodwinked, given to run riot in idolatries, drifting into vanities, congregating in absurdities, planning short-sightedly, plotting dementedly; whenever they are at variance with their professions, and violate the unwritten but perceptible laws binding them in consideration one to another; whenever they offend sound reason, fair justice; are false in humility or mined with conceit, individually, or in the bulk; the Spirit overhead will look humanely malign, and cast an oblique light on them, followed by volleys of silvery laughter. That is the Comic Spirit.[17]

In the novels which succeeded the allegorical—at times more precisely symbolic—*Shaving of Shagpat,* 1855, Meredith was to let his various comic adventurers typify one or more of the apostasies from truth and virtue which require the laughter of the comic spirit. They were to take their places in an over-all design in which they might be dominant or only subsidiary. But in the beginning the novelist took all folly for his province and, in his symbolic tapestry, wove a fabric of the bright hues of comedy with a contrasting pattern of tragic shade. *The Shaving of Shagpat,* with its supernatural phenomena, describes nothing short of the transcending of illusion itself, of that illusion which makes man idolatrous, at variance with his professions, false in humility, and bombastical. Though Meredith once spoke against the finding of detailed allegory in the romance, he later approved Mr. James McKechnie's so interpreting it, and, in fact, he very definitely indicated by choral and other comments what were the symbolic character defects of his hero, Shibli Bagarag. His incidents were, indeed, little more than nineteenth-century folkways dressed in the trappings of Arabian-Night romance and transferred from the drawing rooms of England to the magic carpets of Bagdad.

The loose framework of an oriental tale gave Meredith the freedom to invent whatever incidents would illustrate his thoughts. The events have an appearance of a sportive frisking of fancy, with anything acceptable to the author which catches his whim, whether it be cockleshell boats, roc's-egg bridges, swords which extend to sightless length, or a hair rising from a man's head to a height above the housetops, flaming blindingly, and hurling its attackers away with a magical shock. But it is in this seemingly disjointed and fantastic concatenation that the novelist established the essential theme and pattern of a Meredithian novel. Egoism and illusion or, more precisely, the illusion with which we seek to clothe our egos against reality is the antagonist, and the unifying theme is its mastery. Because such illusion can sometimes be overcome only at the price of tragedy, Meredith inserted the story of Bhanavar the Beautiful, to which we shall have to return for the underlying themes of his tragedies. In the rest of his narrative he had critical fun with the rebellious refusal of Shibli Bagarag to come to terms with duty and truth. In discussing some of the incidents McKechnie has shown how aptly in the realm of ideas the events fit sequently together. For our study here it is perhaps best to think of the book as exploring a wilderness of ideas with special concern for the innumerable false paths, where, if one escapes the tragic bogs, he may still wander all night in pursuit of the goblin Jack and his lantern.

To turn from the order of the telling to the chronology of the events themselves, we begin with the Identical—the hair that symbolizes illusion—in the possession of the genie Karaz. Karaz is not per se evil, but he is devoid of spiritual good. He is a constantly active power, as active as man's mind, and he cannot be destroyed. Noorna, whom Meredith presents as Duty, supremely beautiful and deeply human, but ensorcelled into a hag, has perceived that with the Identical in his possession Karaz is a sinister being, and so she has sought to strip from him illusion which would give evil direction to his cunning. But unfortunately the Identical exists as an entity which stern duty alone cannot destroy, and Noorna, unable to kill illusion, has sought to make it passive by planting it in the head of the lethargic and stupid Shagpat. Her attempt to neutralize, however, does not succeed, because the once inconspicuous Shagpat becomes a hero to his city and his city a model for others, and Karaz himself is no less dangerous than before, as he is still controlled by a sorceress.

This condition, to judge from his later comedies, is what Meredith found in nineteenth-century Europe. Into it he introduces a knight-errant as enthusiastic as the later Beauchamp and as naïve as Beauchamp, Evan Harrington, or Harry Richmond, or, as the novelist would admit, as naïve as himself and Everyman. Shibli Bagarag sees life as an adventure. He has heard of the Identical and, like Spenser's Red Cross Knight, he has not a hesitant thought in welcoming the quest. He loves the good and the beautiful and scorns the evil and ugly. He is willing to accept Noorna despite her unbeautiful appearance, for she offers help and, besides, championing her will attest to his own nobility. In fact, he soon comes up against many egoistic temptations and the actual shaving of Shagpat is no longer exciting for its own sake. What keeps Shibli eager is the thought of the inevitable reward; he will be a hero. Shagpat will be dethroned and Shibli will become the cynosure. The guerdon is so delightful that he luxuriates in its anticipation, even as Mart Tinman, in *The House on the Beach,* is later to strike his court poses before his mirror and bask in her majesty's expected praise. We perceive at once, of course, that the Identical by its magical properties is really growing gigantically in Shibli's own head. He is the grandsire of all the Meredithian sentimentalists, including some otherwise worthy, who think not of the act but of the glory they will receive when they have performed it.

With cryptic lines which set the design of the Book of

Egoism, the Pilgrim's Scrip, and the various other sources of maxims, Shibli's progress in folly is recorded in axioms:

> Who seeks the shadow to the substance sinneth . . .
> He, waxing liker to what he pursueth,
> Himself becometh what he chased in vain!

The consequence of his first delusion is a vigorous thwacking. But he is slow to learn and the shadow persists in returning to him. What is worse, he tends to resemble the various evils which he turns aside to destroy. At times he can be honest in analyzing his position and his error, as in his lament of humiliation:

> To be the first of men I aim
> And find myself the least.

The complaint does not, however, presage renunciation. It is poignant with egoism which repeated thwackings cannot quite destroy.

Only Shagpat possesses the Identical, but all men where his fame has gone refuse to be shaved. They have no Identical to lose, but they fearfully protect their outward resemblance to the revered one, as anxiously, we may say, as the conventional English gentleman adhered to whatever fallacies tradition had caused to prevail. An audacious barber who would heretically snip the magic hair is himself susceptible, of course, to a never-ending variety of his own illusions. At the moment when Shibli thinks that he has conquered one, scores of new forms spring up in its place. He once peeps beneath the veil of Rabesqurat, Queen of the Enchanted Lake and Mistress of Illusions, and the bold act discovers her hideous reality and almost denudes her of her power. But she recovers and musters a phantasia of deceptions to confuse him. Appealing to his love of glory, she entices him to luxuriate in a dream of power, with Rabesqurat herself as his queen. When the Event approaches, she creates hundreds of Shagpats, so that Shibli strikes wildly, destroying buildings with the mad recklessness of a desperate reformer. Only by putting the Sword of Aklis, that is, the light of the intellect, "between the first and second thought" in her head does he dissipate her malice. Thereafter, Meredith tells us, she "is no longer mighty, for the widening of her power has weakened it, she being now the mistress of the single-thoughted, and them that follow one idea to the exclusion of a second."

Of the many things which Shibli must do before he can gain possession of the Sword of Aklis and can master its stroke, one is of particular interest, because it affronts the idealism of a corrector of the world's ills and thus is later a baffling vexation to Beauchamp. Noorna, who is responsible for Shibli's thwackings and can also nurse him when he has nothing but a sense of duty to cling to, can also give him practical counsel. Having summoned the genie Karaz and, despite his terrifying aspect, forced him to assume the form of an ass, she commands Shibli to mount him in pursuit of his mission. As she remarks, quoting "the poet":

"It is the sapiency of fools
To shrink from handling evil tools."

Karaz is not a docile ass, and there is no pretense that duty has transformed him into a domestic burden carrier who will munch his oats gratefully at the caravanserai of cynical sentimentality. He will, in fact, as the creature of Rabesqurat, return in many avatars, at times plucking at eyes to prevent their perceiving illusion, or even becoming that especially Meredithian plaguer, the flea, which can make the most sublime intention give way to a travesty of scratching and slapping. But for a little while Shibli must use him. The risk is great, but fortunately for Shibli, Noorna does not let him conceal from himself the nature of the beast he rides upon.

Unlike the old-style politicians of *Beauchamp's Career,* he never is permitted to fall asleep in the saddle in lethargic indifference to the relation of means to end.

None of the magical fantasies which delay Shibli are far-fetched if we think of the strange ways of the human mind, but three of his adventures are particularly close to actuality and reappear without much change in Meredith's later fiction. They all take place in the Palace of Aklis and are so inter-related that one blends with another. In the Palace there are beasts' heads on men and men's heads on beasts. The symbolism is, of course, not novel. Yet for a writer who was trying to bring into accord the intellectual and the physical natures of man the Circean tradition had fresh implications. Shibli, already tempted by Rabesqurat to imagine himself a monarch, is welcomed by these strange men-beasts and is crowned and enthroned. His crown is composed of "bejewelled asses' ears stiffened upright, and skulls of monkeys grinning with gems." To pay him homage, asses, monkeys and other ridiculous creatures are brought in. Though slightly dismayed by his subjects, he picks one to be his vizier and reflects that all men are ruled like these. The satiric overtones are audible. Among the suggestions is the comic irony of hero worship. Shibli is made king because he is a hero, but society demands of its heroes that they forsake all the originality which has made them superior to their fellows and become the enslaved idols of conformity. Meredith may not have had specific examples in mind; it is noteworthy, however, that his later references to Tennyson as the popular seer identify his popularity with his submssion to conventional and commonplace sentiment, and that he himself scoffed at pleasing popular reviewers. The flattery of one's fellows was not only a temptation to the ego for self-glorification; it was a lazy mind's refuge from the need for courageous, independent thinking.

There are also among Shibli's devotees a multitude of beautiful damsels, much more charming, in fact, than the ladies of various ages who are to adore Sir Willoughby and Sir Austin or to obtain simultaneously business guidance and brotherly sympathy from Victor Radnor. In other respects, however, they are very similar. It has sometimes been felt in the twentieth century that Tennyson's Sir Galahad is a prig in refusing to respond to ladies' smiles because his heart is set on the Grail. Actually, inasmuch as he does enjoy the devotion, Galahad expresses the epitome of that sentimental gilding of sensuality which Meredith was repeatedly to deplore. That the knight does not single out one of the ladies who cast their eyes upon him and attempt to seduce her does not lessen the charge. By the novelist's standard he would still be guilty of desire for possession without responsibility, and it would not matter that this did not involve physical expression, There was for Meredith a sentimental harem just as sensual as a physical one. It is this kind which Shibli finds in the Hall of Maidens in the Palace of Aklis. In generosity to Tennyson we shall assume that he did not let his own mind linger irresponsibly on Galahad's image of the doting ladies. Meredith's comic protagonists, including Shibli, are less fortunate. The quest for the Identical—a quest bearing resemblances to that for the Grail—suddenly vanishes from Shibli's thoughts as, like Tennyson's Gawain, he lingers among his flock. But, as with the asses and monkeys, he is ironically trapped. The luxury of his carefree possession is but a brief illusion. Like Sir Austin and the others, he discovers himself helpless; the damsels have no wish to free him from the trammels of their devotion.

It is the bitter aftertaste of sentimental adoration which is to convert Sir Austin to the sentimentality of cynicism, and the vulgar fawning of beasts with men's heads is to turn Fleetwood's thoughts to contempt for mankind. The third temptation of Shibli follows the same pattern. The transformed creatures, he is told, were once men who, like him, sought the Sword, but "plunged into the tank of temptation" by yielding to "the lures of vanity, the blinding of ambition, and tasting the gall of the Roc." The Voice of Aklis stresses the folly of gall tasting, that is, of cynicism, by announcing that the shaving of Shagpat would be "a service to mankind ranking next my vanquishing of the Roc." In Meredith's allegory vanquishing an evil does not mean rendering it powerless over others; the Roc is still alive and it is only by the most cautious traversal of the bridge of its eggs that Shibli escapes falling victim to the bird itself and becoming tragically comic. There was no place in Meredith's philosophy for cynical gall. To evince contempt for one's fellows was to divorce oneself from the heritage of civilization in which alone the spirit could prosper; to become bitter about life itself was to renounce the miraculous nature of intelligence and become a beast-headed man.

Laughter is the specific. It is when Shibli sees himself in a mirror and laughs that he is free to descend from the throne. Later, when he sees the bewitched men and remembers that he has been like them, he laughs again, and his crown falls from his head onto that of a monkey. If the others could but laugh too, he perceives, they would cast off their enchantment. But they are like the men bewitched earlier by Goorelka, who were "denied the privilege of laughter" though their folly was "matter for laughter." Shibli has not caused enchantments to cease to exist, but he has learned to live among them. His eventual severing of the Identical is a personal triumph; its social benefit is temporary—"for the mastery of an Event lasteth among men the space of one cycle of years, and after that a fresh Illusion springeth to befool mankind." In fact, of the reign of the new king, Shibli's uncle, Baba Mustapha, in the City of Oolb—which has taken its fashions from the City of Shagpat—Meredith remarks with the concluding words of the book, ". . . there is matter therein for the amusement of generations."

Though in the form of a chivalric quest, Shibli's story is essentially one of rebellion against the truth. He cannot until the end bring himself to discard all the illusions which prevent the free play of intellect. Only at the end does he completely forget himself; in the enthusiasm of swinging his sword he lives intensely—as intensely as any novelist might in his own delight in the exercise of the comic spirit. It is the intellectual excitement that liberates him from his egoistic bewitchment and lets him take all man's spiritual heritage as his own.

In the flexible narrative pattern of the story Shibli wanders from one episode to another and recalls the tragic tale of Bhanavar or hears the comic anecdote of the builder Khipil, who, having pretended that his structure was complete, was forced to walk its non-existent floor; and Shibli's adventures are supplemented by those of Baba Mustapha, who, in his suffering the torment of the flea and in his revery of power and sensual pleasure, is a burlesque imitation of Shibli. The Arabian-Night structure of the narrative merely foreshadows the method which Meredith was to feel quite free to follow in his later novels. The theme itself was the criterion of unity. The novelist was to explore its various aspects, however often he might need to stop the progress of his main plot and follow the theme through some ramification.

After pursuing in *Farina,* 1857, the romantic exhilaration of love and adventure, which had its counterpart too in the fabulous incidents of Shibli's career, Meredith turned to *The Ordeal of Richard Feverel.* In it and in most of his novels thereafter he interwove the strands of romance, comedy, tragedy, and tragicomedy with an experimenter's audacity. From 1859, when the first version of *The Ordeal* appeared, through 1876, with *Beauchamp's Career,* whatever else a novel might relate, part, and often the main part, of its action was devoted to the education of one of various Shibli Bagarags. Their lives might end in tragedy or in inability to find the way out of the Hall of Aklis, and they might be clothed in romance; but in any event they were to be illuminated by the impartial light of comedy. Richard, Evan, Edward Blancove, Wilfrid Pole, Harry Richmond, and Beauchamp are all comic in their determined championing of illusion, in their refusal to look in a mirror and see their true selves. Though Edward is unable to rise to the pitch of romantic enthusiasm which even Wilfrid twice or thrice achieves, he is sufficently chastened by tragedy to deserve rank with the rest, above the ass-eared man-beasts and the hypocritical sensualists whose ignoble lives are never purified by either laughter, tragedy, or romance.

There is good fun in *Farina,* whose hero is so much an idealist that, when contrasted with his practical friend, the Goshawk, he is discovered to be quixotically incomplete, afraid to handle "evil tools." But he is not nearly so fully analyzed as the heroes to follow. His comic incongruities are depicted in the realm of medieval romance, with its supernatural accouterments, and so merely continue the method of *The Shaving of Shagpat.* But with *The Ordeal* Meredith turned from the world of symbols, where the reader must supply the actual, to the world of actuality, where, with hints by the author, he discovers the symbolic.

The boyish vanities of Richard, some of which Meredith curtailed in revision, need not concern us here. It is with the advent of the love season, that is, the eating of the "shaddock," (cf. *infra.,* page 148) that the carnival of egoism really begins. Richard is at first transported to the mountain tops of romance, but he soon descends to the plain of vanities and then to the sloughs of sentimental sensuality. As Lucy's husband he expects her to trust his wisdom, yet he accuses her of lack of courage. Here we have the egoistic concept of woman as a passive "fortress." It is Lucy, of course, who is really brave, as she has given her happiness into the hands of a rash young man who knows neither her mind nor his own.

Having tasted the shaddock, Richard is ready for the supreme of vanities. He understands women, he is sure, and leaving his wife protected by her devotion to him and by her innocence, he sets out with his friend Ripton as a knight-errant champion of women in distress. Actually, Lucy is most in distress, and it is not mere innocence or devotion that saves her, but rather good sense and courage. Inspired by the alluring prospect of converting Mountfalcon to virtue, she never loses sight of her mission and, though unsuccessful in it, she herself escapes seduction. Meanwhile Richard is talking virtue to Mrs. Mount(falcon), whose husband has bribed her to seduce him. His motives are pure; he has rescued his own mother, whose desertion of Sir Austin has brought her wretchedness, and he assures the bewitching fallen woman before him that he will not himself fall, but will raise her up. "Old hypocrites talk in that way," she muses, "but I never heard of a young man doing it, and not making love at the same time."

Henceforth Bella, not Richard, plays the active role, a part which Meredith's egoists always consider masculine, but which they invariably surrender in crises. It is when she dresses like a man and when she quotes from *Othello,* wishing "that heaven had made her such a man," that Richard is most ensnared. His desire to save her does not exclude all other feelings: "The mighty pity falling from his eyes took in her whole shape. She did not mistake it for tenderness." With the cry "O Bella! let me save you" he capitulates, and the chapter ending again echoes Shakespeare with an ironic twist: "Was ever hero in this fashion won?"

Bella's love for Richard does save her, but her salvation is entirely her own doing. Before continuing on his career, which will include some tragicomedy and much tragedy that is not comic, Richard has lingered long enough in the Hall of Maidens to become like that which he sought to destroy. Unfortunately, though Mrs. Mount's drawing room is beautifully appointed, it has no mirrors for the soul, and Richard, who could, years before, laugh at himself, must now drink the gall of the Roc.

Because the Shaddock Dogma is central in the theme of *The Ordeal,* the novel has an ample complement of sensualists. Of these some are guilty of yet more serious sins which pertain to tragedy, but they belong none the less with the sensualists too. In the first version Adrian, the Wise Youth, has been having a clandestine affair with Farmer Blaize's servant, and she once twits him on his hypocritical austerity. In the revision he is discreetly cautious in his purchased loves, but he is still a ridiculous gallant when he pats Lucy's hand and tries to win her affection. Like Adrian, Berry, who has deserted his wife, is a lady's man among the servants and is confident of his prowess. His wife continues to love him until she sees him again and discovers that she neither needs nor cares for him; with that discovery he is absurdly unimportant. Mountfalcon, the first of several Meredithian rakes, is a good example of the author's comic insight. He has bought women's favors, and his marriage has been a loveless purchase; but he has achieved therefrom no bolstering of his insecure ego. To win Lucy would be a triumph, and he uses all his clumsy wiles, even to dramatizing himself as a wicked man yearning for salvation. Away from her he can condemn Richard for infidelity to so pure and saintly a wife and then suddenly swear with fury because she does not yield herself to him. He is a pre-Freudian study of the possibility that sexual prowess may be the recourse of persons who have no other chance of success; and his helpless fury exposes him as a permanent resident among the asses and monkeys of Aklis. Sandoe, the seducer of Richard's mother, has been given to sensuality too and has gone on to the second and third stages in its expression, "for being inclined to vice, and occasionally, and in a quiet way, practicing it, he was of course a sentimentalist and a satirist." Because he once offered the appearance of glamor and provided escape from Sir Austin, Richard's mother joined him, only to have to assume the role of protector as Sandoe deteriorated into tawdry effeteness.

All these men are egoists and in their various ways sentimentalists. But none are quite so comically guilty as Sir Austin himself. His tragic relations with Richard will concern us elsewhere; his cruelty to women is worse than that of Mountfalcon, who usually settles for their bodies. We do not care for the several harems of women who, particularly in the first version, have thrown themselves at his feet, but Lady Blandish deserves better. It is in the Pilgrim's Scrip that Sir Austin defines for Meredith a key term—"Sentimentalists . . . are they who seek to enjoy without incurring the Immense Debtorship for a thing done." Lady Blandish has yet to learn the ironic truth of the Scrip when the chapter ends:

> "My wound has healed," he said. "How?" she asked. "At the fountain of your eyes," he replied, and drew the joy of new life from her blushes, without incurring further debtorship for a thing done.

Though Mrs. Berry was speaking only from her own marital experience, she would seem to have generalized rather soundly when she told Richard, "But all men are men."

Evan Harrington's mother has a Port; his dead father, the Great Mel, had a Presence. Evan's own mental history, as we discover, is the comic rivalry between the two forces which the words connote. There are in the novel other symbolic devices which enhance its charm as a romance, but essential to the comedy is Evan's heritage. He is only half his father's son and cannot escape from his mother's pedestrian world of duty; and yet he cannot renounce his love for Rose Jocelyn to sign himself tailor and pay his father's debts. He must therefore make and remake mistakes and submit to sound and humiliating thwackings.

Evan is physically brave, but in a world that stamps a value on family rank and stigmatizes useful employment he has lacked moral courage and insight. Like his sisters, he has tried to imitate his father's social success; but whereas Mel could fit trousers on a lord and the same evening dine at the lord's table, Evan, while yet at school, has called himself a gentleman. Later he realizes that a gentleman is one who, of whatever rank, is noble in conduct, and he can then see himself superior to many of his aristocratic associates. But his argument at once exposes his vanity; since character is what matters, he is determined to compel these inferiors to accept him as their social equal. His reasoning calls to mind that of Steele's duelist. Meredith, who appears to have drawn heavily on his own sensations as a tailor's grandson, can laugh at him, but never with scorn.[18] With Charles Lamb, he understood that snobbery in a spirited youth was inseparable from his spiritedness and that only his own laughter could restore such a lad after the sharp blows to his sensibilities.

Evan is not a diamond with a rough exterior. He is, rather, a moderately intelligent and imaginative fellow, bred to no useful employment; and, apart from skill in swimming, some talent in horseback riding, and an acceptable air in a drawing room, he has no accomplishments. He is a very average lad, who does heroic things when he does not stop to think, but has no developed convictions:

> Are you impatient with this young man? He has little character for the moment. Most youths are like Pope's women; they have no character at all. And indeed a character that does not wait for circumstances to shape it, is of small worth in the race that must be run.

He does not learn quickly, but one shortcoming sometimes helps him to see another. Death and funerals were solemn matters in Victorian literature, yet at Mel's death Meredith not only found comedy in Mrs. Mel's scorn for tear-shedding women, but he made Evan's journey home a comic chastisement of vanity. Having started in a chariot, he must dismount impoverished to submit to the postillion's insolence:

> Pride was the one developed faculty of Evan's nature . . . From the vague sense of being an impostor, Evan awoke to the clear fact that he was likewise a fool.

Circumstance has given Port momentary victory over Presence.

Pathos is, of course, essential to Evan's growth, even as it was to Shibli's. When he first meets Susan Wheedle and learns of her desertion, he perceives that there is "something more abhorrent than sitting with one's legs crossed." Later, his deep concern for his sister Caroline and his pity for the dying Juliana Bonner give emotional depth to his new sense of values. When he meets Susan, however, he is hardly beyond the outset of his education. Generously and proudly he insists on paying her bills, already guaranteed by Tom Cogglesby, and once more poverty must cast the victory to Port. It is now that Evan aggressively assumes the defensive. Presence and ale make him offer to fight a duel upon the insults of Harry Jocelyn and his companions, but Port makes him admit he is a tailor, and to unsay the tailordom would be to substitute coward. The consequence is that Evan is no longer able to move forward and must helplessly yield the generalship to his sister the Countess de Saldar, who would prefer cowardice to tailordom but hopes prevarication will avoid both; and to Rose, who cannot believe that he is a tailor, then has to believe, and though she cannot say *snips* in the mirror without a wry face, sets out to make her lover socially acceptable. Evan is now indeed very much "second fiddle."

Port is as repellent as Noorna was ugly; and tailordom is a hideous Demogorgon:

> He saw the squalid shop, the good, stern, barren-spirited mother, the changeless drudgery, the existence which seemed indeed no better than what the ninth of a man was fit for.

When Evan does yield to duty and bid farewell to Rose, he overplays his humility to win her disbelief in its cause: "He tried to be honest, and was as much so as his disease permitted." There is refuge in letting Rose misconstrue and in letting her and the Countess manage: "Of course Evan knew that he was managed." He shies from mastering the Event and for a long while continues the feminine role. But pride cannot endure it without anguish:

> To play second fiddle to a young woman is an abomination to us all. . . . If we are to please you rightly, always allow us to play First.

Only the arrival of Mrs. Mel with the announcement that Evan is a tailor rescues him from complete enslavement in the Hall of Maidens.

In his rationalizations he confuses Rose's welfare with his own and must for her sake keep up pretense. Meredith reminds us of the symbolic nature of his dilemma:

> The little imps pluck at you: the big giant assails you: the seductions of the soft-mouthed siren are not wanting. Slacken the knot an instant, and they will all have play. And the worst is, that you may be wrong, and they may be right!

For resolution of the conflict Evan must come to terms with Port; and yet, since the story is of romantic comedy, Presence must not sacrifice the things of the imagination. To make the justice poetic Evan, having proved himself a true gentleman, must propose and be accepted within the shop, which he will then be free to abandon. But for this denouement is needed the pathos, the relentless severity of Mrs. Mel, the comic fairy-godfather intercession of old Tom Cogglesby, and above all the determined courage of Rose, who once tells her uncle Melville, "And *I'm* not going to be bred up to go into a harem, you may be sure." It is true that when she says those words she has her arm around her uncle's neck and is flattering him as if he were a sultan, and she is later about to submit to a harem existence as the wife of Laxley; but when Evan does finally master the Event, it is she who steadies the shears. When we remember that she resembles her strong-minded mother and that her father has years ago become second fiddler, we foresee no sudden revolution for Evan.

To give perspective by showing the difference between actual upper-class life and Evan's glamorous illusion, Meredith introduced a gallery of effete, inept, and sensual persons, and he had sport with the affectations of the upper classes. Rose's father is a nonentity; her uncle Melville, a statesman, is ridiculous—his balance of power being of less practical value than tailor Goren's new balance in the seat of trousers; her brother Harry carousingly drinks to Susan's baby, not knowing that it is his own, and he is utterly foolish when the Countess de Saldar inflates him into a Don Juan and then corrects his boorish manners; the family guest, the duke, is a would-be seducer; and Laxley is a dull, wooden lover. The family themselves look forward to Juliana's early death to get her inheritance, and they are as defensively comic in their fear of declining socially as the Harringtons are in their efforts to rise. With these characters filling in the pattern the novel is nevertheless essentially on Evan's reluctance, like that of Shibli, to reconcile the dream with the reality. The resolution of his conflict is not the less pertinent that it is presented in comedy, involving Presence and Port, instead of its usual tragic form.

In *Sandra Belloni,* 1864, Meredith once again blended romance, comedy, and tragedy. Emilia (Sandra) herself is the romantic touchstone by which the comic actions of others are tested. This time it is the false refinement of civilization that is stripped bare, principally in the lives of Wilfrid Pole and his three sisters. The lives of Adela, Arabella, and Cornelia Pole include pathos, but never tragedy, for no matter how frustrated their hopes may be, even if a lover commits suicide, they will not face the disaster frankly and with passion, but will take refuge as always in the "Fine Shades" and "Nice Feelings." They and Wilfrid are "little people," as Meredith reminds us, but he adds that little people when not on guard are "humankind naked." The comedy in their actions is that they evince mainly negative inhibitions of civilization and none of the freedom of spirit which it should presumably bring: "Civilized little people are moved to fulfil their destinies and to write their histories as much by distaste as by appetite." In the midst of romance, they cannot enjoy it because they have not the gusto that ignores trivial defects. When, for example, the girls, typed by the author as Pole, Polar, and North Pole, first hear Emilia singing, they like her song but notice her untied boot-lace. They are indeed painfully susceptible to Karaz as flea.

When Cornelia wants to ask Wilfrid whether Lady Charlotte would not be mercenary in marrying him, she cannot meet the issue directly, but in the language of the fine shades alludes to the fact that Charlotte is "much older" than he. Though her manner is typical of all three, she and her sisters are not burlesques. They scheme desperately and play a double game in their concern to marry against paternal wishes and yet not wound their father. They do not greatly love him and they are disturbed that his grammar is not "parental," but they must conform to an idealized pattern of filial devotion. At one time Cornelia would actually welcome her father's financial ruin that she might marry her impoverished lover, Barrett; yet she must seem loyal to Pole, who hopes she will win the uninteresting gray-headed Sir Twickenham Pryme. Afraid to come face to face with difficulties, the girls at first believe that only indirect allusions and a studied manner can get for them social success and good marriages, which they need for self-respect; and later, when success is virtually abandoned, they are still playing determinedly the same game to avoid what they would consider disgrace. At the end they are deeper and deserving of sympathy; indeed Meredith reminds us along the way that they are "to emerge considerably shorn, but purified—examples of one present passage of our civilization." Yet when Barrett has committed suicide, Adela must ask Wilfrid to influence Cornelia to quit wearing black because, though Sir Twickenham, slighted by Cornelia, has turned to Adela, he would flee if there were gossip that Cornelia had jilted him from devotion to the memory of Barrett. Adela is thus resorting to the fine shades to get a lover, even a second-hand and hare-hearted one, without wounding her sister. It is this type of predicament that the girls have always been in, because they are helplessly dependent on their father, an impractical investor, and because they belong to a civilization in which there is not the wildest dream of their striking out on a career for themselves.

Like his sisters, Wilfrid is both a victim of his civilization and a contributor to its defects. As a gentleman he has become a soldier and fought in India. Now unoccupied in England, he eventually decides to join the Austrians against Italy, not from principle but mainly for Lady Charlotte's approbation. His sisters have at first exploited the glamor of his being wounded and almost getting a medal in India, but they are distressed because he has no intellectual accomplishments. He is a sentimentalist, and he can never for long rid himself of self-conscious apprehensions. Having ably defended Emilia during a rustic fist fight, he is embarrassed by the damage to his face. When Emilia tells of her childhood poverty and of her living mainly on potatoes, Wilfrid's delicacy is affronted; he has already reasoned that he must not fall in love with "a little unformed girl." When they first kiss, it is Wilfrid who draws away; in the conversation which follows he is "quite unaware" that he has chosen the "feminine part." He loves Emilia, but his passion has been dissipated by his effort to reassure himself that she is ladylike in her refinement. He revels in the picture of her as a successful singer in love with him, but when she tells him that she would like to do something to please him, he answers, "When? Where? What with?"

Though Lady Charlotte does not meet his fastidious requirements in person or manner, he has accepted his father's money in order to marry her, and he is consequently tied to her wishes. Yet he is momentarily pleased with what he would otherwise dislike, his father's prospective ruin, because it may free him from his moral commitment. When Emilia rejects his double-dealing plot to keep their love secret, Wilfrid puts on her the masculine task of undeceiving Pole. Without the remotest inclination toward villainy, he plays fast and loose, because he compares the worst feature of one choice with the worst of another and cannot bring himself to positive action: "He could pledge himself to eternity, but shrank from being bound to eleven o'clock on the morrow morning." Early in the story Meredith reminds us of his hero's essential weakness: "Wilfrid was young, and under the dominion of his senses; which can be, if the sentimentalists will believe me, as tyrannous and misleading when super-refined as when ultra-bestial."

Because throughout his career, which continues in a minor but basically unchanged form in *Vittoria,* Wilfrid is never trapped by his indecision into a moment of rashness or into significant melancholy, he escapes tragicomedy. He also, however, misses true heroism. Having planned a romantic interception of Emilia's carriage, he cannot act swiftly to carry her off, but, discovered by her companions, murmurs, "Too late," and retires. Not a sensualist in the obvious manner, he is comic precisely because the mastery of his sensual over his mental nature is disguised even from Wilfrid himself. Like his sisters, he is one of "the finer beings who labour under these excessive sensual subtleties." "I perceive their uses," the novelist continues, "and they are right good comedy. . . . Man is the laughing animal. So let us be cordially thankful to those who furnish matter for sound embracing laughter."

In his castigation of sentimentality Meredith suggests that sentimentalism is the nineteenth-century substitute for monasticism, a point he was to explore years later when he let his tragicomic sentimentalist Fleetwood enter a monastery. He recalls for us that we still have tails though the sentimentalists deny them, and it is Wilfrid's attempt at denial of the animal in him that makes for incongruity. He would have a mistress of the affections without stooping to uncouthness or physical seduction and without assuming debtorship, but he is afraid of Emilia because to a talented singer he can only play second fiddle. When he once mistakenly thinks he can forgive her, he is happy, because then he is the magnanimous hero. In his subsequent enthusiasm Wilfrid writes her a love note, "but even in the red heat of passion his born diplomacy withheld his own signature." Of the many ludicrous incidents, one of the most pointed clearly typifies the sentimentalist. About to be self-forgetful, if not heroic, in again chasing Emilia's carriage, Wilfrid unfortunately runs into a pot boy, most certainly the agent of Karaz if not the genie himself, and is doused with beer. To counteract the odor he sprinkles himself liberally with Alderman's Bouquet perfume. Instead of accepting the truth and finding in it laughter or romance, Wilfrid and the other little people shrink into a sentimental world of make-believe and dissipate their nervous energy in its timid defense. They are not great lost souls in Limbo, but rather the sterile half-spirits of a negative civilization. They can never master the Event.

Edward Blancove, in *Rhoda Fleming,* 1865, escapes the charge of being a villain because in taking Dahlia as his mistress and then paying to have her married to another he must answer to the worse charge of being a sentimental fool. Very much a creature of his sensations, he has been drawn by Dahlia's unreserved admiration of him, but he is soon distressed by her lack of sophistication. He hopes by travel and by reading poetry, for which he has a dilettante condescension, to transform her into a peer of the fascinating Mrs. Lovell. At no time has he any interest in her thoughts or feelings or in her history. She is at first a charming novelty and then suddenly an obstacle to his hypothetical public career. Subservient to a father who wants him to marry riches, he deceives Dahlia so long as her presence flatters him, for as an egoist he fully welcomes enjoyment without responsibility. He will have pleasure, yet be free to pursue his career.

The comic irony is, of course, that Edward is not free at all. Though he foolishly believes that Mrs. Lovell admires his brains and his courage, he is so afraid to face the consequences of his folly that he flees to France and takes refuge in pretending that the money he gives his cousin Algy as his agent will get Dahlia happily married. Later, when he perceives that he has done wrong, he would still have the luxury of Dahlia's forgiving him and throwing herself into his arms. His life has been, in fact, a constant alternation of distasteful sensations of the actual—as in the bleak lodging-house rooms, where he is repelled by the cheerless atmosphere to which he consigns Dahlia—and dreams of success and pleasure. A detailed record of his actions would show that at a lower, more depressing level than that of Wilfrid he flees from one unpleasant sensation only to experience a worse one. Whatever limited cunning he possesses is never put to work by malice or wrath, but always by a fear of committing himself to eleven o'clock the next morning.

Edward's story does have a mildly triumphant ending. When Dahlia finally consents to speak to him, though she cannot love him, he gains some recognition of her maturity, and he will remain celibate and true to her in expiation. Never having had a career, he has none now, and his devotion is a histrionic shadow of monkish steadfastness. But though he cannot be expected to strip his ego naked of all its sentimental raiment, Dahlia has made him as good a person as he is capable of becoming. The dissipated force of his fragile passion has been gathered up into a single impulse which for so negative a person is almost heroic.

Though Meredith was exploring through the actions of his titular heroine, Rhoda, the sins of the intellect for which ultimately social mores were responsible, he found use for a character the antithesis of Rhoda, who would never err from adherence to narrow Puritan principles, but would typify a life of animal instinct with no principles whatever. In Algernon Blancove he created so alluring an example that he could not bring himself to remember proportions. Indeed, like Shakespeare's clowns, Meredith's sometimes insist on saying more than should have been set down for them. Of Algernon's pertinence for the Comic Spirit the author writes:

> Nay, the most worthless creatures are most serviceable for examination when the microscope is applied to them, as a simple study of human mechanism. This youth is one of great Nature's tom fools; an elegant young gentleman outwardly, of the very large class who are simply the engines of their appetites, and, to the philosophic eye, still run wild in woods, as did the primitive nobleman that made a noise in the earlier world.

The son of a squire, Algernon is unaccomplished and useless. For his blunders he chides fate and society, and though he would be utterly helpless without friends, he dreams of freedom and success, which he can have whenever he chooses to start afresh in Australia. Algernon is not by nature eager to be malicious. His superstition demands that he be generous before gambling, and when he has not enough money to dine as a lord, he is likely to give away coppers until he must borrow to dine at all. Gambling, especially at horse races, is, he feels, required of him as a gentleman, and it is as diverting as an occasional day of quiet in the country or a trip to church or the opera. Some of Algy's actions are not per se comic. Eventually he gambles away money that does not belong to him; he tries to get Rhoda as his wife by the power he has to expose her uncle; and worst of all, he would for his own gain marry Dahlia to the villain Sedgett. His comedy is in the fact that he is by nature indolent, loving luxurious ease of body and mind, yet from his sheer animal indolence and refusal to be intellectual he gets himself into conditions that give him no ease and tax his cunning to the limit. When the money is lost or when he has illegally pawned unpaid-for jewelry, he is a rabbit-like creature persecuted by a callous world and forced to use his amoral ingenuity in some new attempt to evade absolute ruin. The employer of Sedgett, he gets into a fist fight with him over the question of his own gentlemanliness and soon finds himself in the scoundrel's toils.

In the hands of a Dreiser, Algernon would steadily deteriorate in character and descend to a tragic ending. Meredith follows him from the folly of vanity down the opportunist path to baseness, and he stresses the fact that a fool can cause evil but never correct it. By maintaining a comic perspective, however, he can reveal not only that Algy's life is a wretched thing but that sensual hedonism in whatever degree or disguise is laughable. A man may glory in villainy or imagine himself a hero suffering from a cruel fate, but unless he has some courage and principles, he cannot endure laughter.

As so often with Meredith, the significant incident is not necessarily the most spectacular; it is the one which displays a trait of character that will determine the other incidents. When Wilfrid was once dejected, he cast himself wildly upon the ground, but he carefully brushed his clothes afterward. When Mrs. Lovell returns Algy's jewels, he does not hurl them through the window as he at first threatens to do, but instead throws them securely into a corner. Such a man is unworthy of a tragic denouement, for he will not even commit folly if it could teach him a lesson; and so instead of sending Algy to jail or to an early suicide, Meredith lets him inherit his father's estate and become a country squire. Though his adolescent years are over—and the author has made much of his youthfulness—we may assume that in his reign as squire, as in that of Baba Mustapha the king, "there is matter . . . for the amusement of generations."

Before he delineated the Egoist himself, Meredith was to have still other flings at comic egoism. Harry Richmond ends his narrative with the comment that he has been a fool and is not yet a philosopher. His story belongs more properly, however, in the realm of romance. In so far as it is comic it parallels Shibli's and especially Evan's conflicts, since Harry is tossed between respect for his practical, unimaginative, and honest grandfather and wonder at his improvident, deluded, yet magnificent father. Beauchamp's career is a romance overflowing with comedy which needs a chapter to itself. Neither youth, however, anticipated so directly as those we have studied the portrait of Willoughby Patterne. Two other heroes, Mart Tinman and General Ople, did. Both men—the one in *The House on the Beach,* 1877, the other in *The Case of General Ople and Lady Camper,* also 1877—are drawn in broad strokes as specimens of vanity. Tinman, once a useful tradesman, would now be a courtier and would also blackmail his former friend into giving him his daughter in marriage. In the comedy of his exposure is the implication that it is the leisure of a would-be gentleman that brings corruption. In the fairy-tale caricature of General Ople the retired officer would above all be "gentlemanly," live in a gentlemanly residence, and do and say only gentlemanly things. By ridicule Lady Camper drives him from his affectation, which has made him a fool and led him to neglect his daughter's security. Though recalling an actual incident, Meredith has given his own twist to it, and Ople's story is to be regarded as a travesty of the idle "gentlemanliness" of his age. In this repect the follies of both Tinman and Ople anticipate the fatuous vanity of Sir Willoughby.

What is it that marks all these characters as citizens of the same kingdom, that is, of the land of Shagpat and Oolb? Certainly they are—all of them—sojourners for a shorter or longer while in the Palace of Aklis, they woo Rabesqurat, acknowledging her for queen, and they are ignobly beset by Karaz, often in his most laugh-provoking embodiment as flea. Every one of them, moreover, would gladly outwit Noorna because she tells him to face the truth. The ass-eared do manage to delude themselves permanently in the belief that they have deceived her; indeed Noorna seems not much to care if they do. But those who have even a little merit are thwacked into submission. And as to the others, their lives furnish not only amusement for generations, but instruction.

Chapter Four

Comedy at Patterne Hall

. . . thy fine unaccented scorn
At sight of man's old secret brute,
Devout for pasture on his prey,
Advancing, yawning to devour;
With step of deer, with voice of flute,
Haply with visage of the lily flower.
(To the Comic Spirit)

THE HERO of early eighteenth-century sentimental literature was not regarded by his creator as a comic figure. When the lord with a bad education in Hughes' little idyll on Amanda writes to her father offering to pay his debts in exchange for securing Amanda as his mistress, he is doing a seriously wicked deed, and only the girl's virtuous beauty in distress purifies him and makes her a lady. Or when Mr. B— discovers in time the beauty of Pamela's virtue and is rescued from his false education to marry her on her own terms, the modern reader's smile is contrary to Richardson's intention; no comedy is meant.

But when Meredith in his most uniformly comic novel, *The Egoist,* in 1879 uses similar motifs and the same excuse for his hero's egoistic wickedness, we laugh with the author and find his story reasonable. For Sir Willoughby Patterne of Patterne Hall has by nature only his normal masculine share of "man's old secret brute"; whatever he shows beyond primitive selfishness is the fault of the civilization which has cherished and spoiled him and which, except for a few brave souls, is determined that he shall not return to a state of nature. As the owner of Patterne Hall he has been encouraged to assume prerogatives for which he has little natural talent and to obscure his instinctive nature by cloaking under polite urbanity defects which should be exposed for correction.

For Hughes and for Cibber and Steele it is sufficient that the hero experience a sudden emotional jolt, which somehow instantly dispels the wicked enchantment and transforms the leering satyr countenance into the features of a virtuous and eligible suitor. For Richardson the process is more intricate, but it is still a thing essentially of the emotions. In each instance the rescue is assumed to be complete. For Meredith the emotions are not irrelevant, but the conversion is primarily intellectual and it can be achieved only at the cost of comic thwackings. Like his Meredithian predecessors, Willoughby is not only cruel but absurd, and it takes many castigations to make him recognize his absurdity. At the end of his progress, when having tried to devour not one but three women, he accepts marriage on an intended victim's own terms, the novelist does not pronounce him cured; in fact, his wife will be mainly alone against society in keeping his ego restrained. But whereas we may fear that Hughes' hero—a character entirely acceptable to Victorian sentimentalists—has perhaps arrived only at that outward appearance of the lily flower which Sir Willoughby has at the beginning, Meredith's hero, who even at the outset is not a crude sensualist, has achieved something more lasting. Without repenting and luxuriating in being forgiven by his victim, he has found that there is something apparently incongruous about his soft deer-like tones with which he has sought to obtain possession without responsibility. He will not rid himself, to be sure, of the brute within, but under Laetitia's critical eye he will not easily disguise it to go forth anew in search of prey.

Since the motif of the comic reformation of a would-be master of women's affections is woven with many other strands in the novel, we can best return to it after looking at other parts of the design. The persistent, though tepid and rarefied, sensuality is indeed only the most prominent of the manifestations of Willoughby's egoism. And egoism itself, whether sensual in expression or not, is of interest mainly as in a negative way it contrasts with and emphasizes the free, imaginative life which Meredith believed to be man's if he could unburden himself of concern for his ego.

In depicting Willoughby's life and the social milieu in which it is fostered, Meredith must have found interest in the artistic problem. Both have a paucity of what the novelist considered worthwhile. With nothing vast in proportions, the social life must run its course of trivial gossip and intrigue, and its central figure must be incapable of heroism because of the deficiency of his imagination. But for Meredith, who could observe that life without being caught up by it and could contrast it with that of his nobler characters, the minute variations of its tensions suggested in comic miniature the sublime and tragic conflicts of the mind.

The setting is the "county." It is the county which is occupied in choosing for Willoughby an acceptable wife, or at least in keeping abreast of his intentions when he threatens to choose his own. It is the county which is astonished upon his sudden departure from England after Constantia has jilted him and which is relieved of boredom when he returns and the scheming can begin anew. There must be many who make up the county, but those who matter are women; and it is Mrs. Mountstuart Jenkinson, seconded and rivalled by Lady Busshe, who establishes the tone. Mrs. Mountstuart is a brilliant woman and she is the mouthpiece for Meredith's thematic aphorisms. But when young she had little to do, and now as a widow she must dissipate her ingenuity in trying to create liveliness where the masculine response is seldom sprightly. For want of better employment she is a patroness seeking amusement. She would like scintillation at her dinner table and so she invites Dr. Middleton and Professor Crooklyn, only to be repaid with crotchety dullness. She has found the physician Dr. Corney amusing, and before the end she carries off his Irish countryman Colonel De Craye with the specific injunction that he must entertain her. But like a lady at court she has to stake her main chance on the reigning sovereign, to build Willoughby into a replica of Louis Quatorze. She is too intelligent to be completely deceived, but at the end she is still conspiring to prevent his losing quite all his tinseled glamor. Though her aphorisms—of which more later—are clever, the sterility of her life reveals how far the "county" has departed from what is natural and useful and intellectually expansive.

In Colonel De Craye Meredith has represented Mrs. Mountstuart's counterpart, the masculine expression of the idle aimlessness of the age. The colonel has a subtle mind but no worthy employment for it. He has found transitory distraction in winning hearts without being himself in love, though he is not by nature a sensual sentimentalist. Of the men in the novel he is the only one who can offer Clara the graceful, witty compliments which indicate an appreciation of her mind and a courtly eagerness to rise to its level. But he is not a working soldier and so has no occupation. He must consent to being patronized by Willoughby and to being told by Mrs. Mountstuart that he will substitute for Corney as what we might call her court jester. De Craye has a serious, indeed slightly melancholy nature; he obtains a little time to compose himself before he re-affixes the mask he is expected to wear. He cannot, however, break from the pattern which is constricting his spirit. He will bow to conformity and by so doing will, like Mrs. Mountstuart, actually intensify the evil which haunts him.

It is in a civilization where Mrs. Mountstuart and De Craye are exceptions in intellectual power, where the average country acquaintance of a baronet subscribes unimaginatively to tradition that the egoist finds his nurture. The comedy is partly in the fact that when he thinks he is most independent he is unwittingly much concerned with his reputation, that when he believes he is most masculine he is actually dominated by women. If Willoughby could fly from his orbit to some magnificent evil, we should not laugh at him. But he keeps all his selfish conduct within safe bounds, where tragedy does not seriously threaten and where the comic imps are free to make merry. The novelist said that he put much of his own self into Sir Willoughby, and any man who pretends not to find himself at all in the baronet is guilty of Willoughby's own naïve belief that he is different from lesser men. The author has given us, in short, a complex theme in which we see both the specific faults of one class and one age and the generic shortcomings of civilized man. It is in his caution, his fears, his refusal to gamble knowingly for high stakes that Willoughby is like most men most of the time. The technical problem was to make such a life interesting.

Meredith went about his task by taking ordinary facts and looking at them with the same imaginative perception that had created the adventures of Shibli Bagarag. The difference in method was only that for Shibli the reader must translate the symbol into fact and with Willoughby one sees the fact grow into a symbol. The baronet, we learn from Mrs. Mountstuart, "has a leg"; more subtly she adds, "You *see* he has a leg." Five pages later Meredith is still having fun with the implications. The elegance of Willoughby's bow is apparent, but the leg itself, the author insists, is eloquent. Willoughby is proud of it as well as of the bow. Long after the novelist has established the picture in our minds we continue to interpret all Willoughby's actions in reference to it. He is not athletic; he expresses no force of character in his legs; he can only attempt to imitate with more refinement than is shown by others the manners that outwardly distinguished the earlier English gentleman, or even more, as Meredith reminds us, the courtier of any time from Louis Treize to Louis Quinze. The leg is a symptom of his illusion. For Willoughby it is identical with feudal and courtly prestige. As the citizens of Oolb all wore beards because one head possessed the Identical, so he will hold to the outward imitation of a nobleman of old. Meredith does not condemn him by burlesque. The baronet is refined; it is only that he is first of all conscious of the appearance he makes in the world, that he can do nothing without his and our being conscious of his leg.

"Reality is the offender," the author tells us, "delusion our treasure that we are robbed of." Willoughby's main delusion is, of course, about his relation to the world. Having refused to accept a limited role in it, he has unconsciously surrendered to its standards. When he tries to resist what he thinks is an encroaching world, that world has already conquered and gone by; and every time he asserts himself Willoughby looks into a mirror, not to see his true self in relation to the world, but only to adjust the posture of his leg.

Because he must maintain his position of dignity the baronet cannot face, still less enjoy, the reality of nature. Young Crossjay, the spirit of precocious boyhood and the symbol of what Willoughby lacks, may exuberantly climb trees to find birds' nests; Vernon Whitford is a hard walker who can fall happily asleep with a book under a tree; and Clara is most charmingly graceful when running a race with Crossjay. But Willoughby, already elderly in his thirty-second year, knows of landscape merely as part of the appropriate design of an estate. He never walks spiritually in a field, for he always brings with him the manner of the drawing room or reconstructs the countryside into an idyllic pastoral setting where the landlord can expect to meet his happy tenants in their holiday mood or their innocent, carefree children. The country is for the egoist necessarily removed from human travail. When he comes upon Laetitia with a group of young girls he condescendingly asks their names, but he hastens to qualify, "Only their Christian names, pray." The girls do not have toiling parents any more than Flitch, whom he dismisses from his service, has nine children to starve. Willoughby has never read enough in history to find whether the landowner ever had an idyllic relation with his tenants or a master's enjoyment of a completely conquered soil. He does not understand that nature rewards only effort with a livelihood and only the adventurous spirit with joy.

Of adventure as a form of reality he can know nothing, even when it cries for recognition. Always blocking his sight of it is concern for the omnipresent leg. A relative in the marines may with a somewhat routine casualness act in the best marine tradition. But the fastidious taste of Sir Willoughby does not want the details. Without them he is the patron of a young madcap, who fights by way of diversion and has an amusing habit of doing things quite heroic, to be sure, but, more importantly, expressive of the romantic Patterne temperament. When the marine is discovered to be a commonplace-looking middle-aged father of several children, the egoist's image is annihilated; and though he sends money and later takes the marine's son as a protégé, he cannot bring himself to explore the reality. We sometimes find that age or illness causes a shrinking from new things; Willoughby's shock upon loss of his illusion is typical of his having missed the age of youth because of his inability to adapt himself to the new. The world he would live in is like a fortress with wooden guns. He cannot sally from it to capture new lands, and when a wall is breached he can only retreat to the keep.

Of learning as an avenue to reality the baronet is also mainly ignorant and even afraid. It is not clear what he has read. He dislikes poetry and resentfully envies those who do not. Possibly Meredith is arbitrary in associating lack of understanding of poetry with egoism; but certainly he is less arbitrary in finding comic Willoughby's dilettante interest in science, for the man's defects will not appear to him during the "never less than an hour" a day he spends in the laboratory when he "can snatch it." Former patrons had their painters and scholars and sometimes their poets. The master of Patterne Hall has Vernon for scholarship and Dr. Middleton for companionship without the intrusion of the learning which a divine ought properly to represent. Science is for him a pretense of modernity. But it is safer than poetry because as he toys with it he has a sense of importance rather than the baffling inferiority that poetry would impose upon him. Meredith did not intend Willoughby's superficial inquiry as a travesty of science, but in his introductory chapter he did protest that his age should not try to make science a cure-all. "Art is the specific," he wrote, for bringing man back to sane, natural ways. It would seem that in the egoist he was attacking the popular superstition that whatever was labeled science must be good. The mere patronage of art would not, of course, help Willoughby, for he would still remain unimaginative and uncreative. So perhaps it is best to take science as the particular form of sterile amusement of a person too busy being a feudal lord to have enthusiasm for any intellectual adventure whatever.

As to the real nature of his social position, to the maintenance of which he is dedicated, Willoughby is utterly deluded. "Feudalism is not an objectionable thing," he once remarks, "if you can be sure of the lord." That he is thinking of himself as the lord comes out when, after perpetrating a series of persecutions, he tells Mrs. Mountstuart, "I really have not a spice of the tyrant in me." The tyranny extends not alone to servants, such as Flitch, but to everyone upon whom the shadow of his imaginary castle falls. Vernon in gratitude for his bounty is expected to let Willoughby dictate his career. Crossjay, eager to enter the navy, is to become a gentleman instead, dependent exclusively on his patron's generosity. Dr. Middleton, because of his lethargy and love of good wine, is a docile parasite, who, like Willoughby's aunts, will encourage feudal patronage and return obedience. Willoughby is so mistaken that he even expects De Craye, a temporary visitor, to give up his individuality and abet his host's marriage scheme. The ironic comedy arises, of course, in the way in which in each instance he is defeated. He is forced by the now-enlightened Laetitia to take Flitch back into service. Having at first planned to make Vernon the counterpart of the olden-time cuckold by bestowing on him his own spiritual mistress, the egoist in mad confusion urges him quite needlessly to accept his intended wife instead. With Vernon and Clara goes Crossjay, and having lost all relish for the flattery of Dr. Middleton once his daughter is gone, Willoughby can only hasten his departure. Mr. Dale, who replaces the doctor, is too ill and too little interested in catering to others to represent an adequate replacement; and De Craye's leaving portends the coming of no new friends now that Clara, his reason for staying, is gone. All that Willoughby has built in order to be the patriarch of a closed community has disintegrated. The others have scurried off to new worlds, leaving him with a depleted domain.

The most serious blows to the egoist's illusion are from women, and the comedy is sharpest when his unimaginative reason wages a losing contest with their highly subtle—Meredith would say poetic—imaginations. It is indeed his lack of ability to see into the minds of others, particularly of women, that makes him in a comic manner experience a moral isolation as desolate as that normally presented in tragedy. In a wife the baronet wants health, money, and beauty. He stipulates the first because illness oppresses him—as it did the hero of Ibsen's *The Doll's House,* also of 1879; his niceness of feeling is disturbed, and, besides, another's illness is a demand on one's attention and sympathy. The money is for prestige, as he has enough of his own, but beauty appeals to his egoism and sensualism alike. It is concerning Willoughby that Meredith states the pronouncement which, as we have seen, applies to his predecessors: "The love-season is the carnival of egoism, and it brings the touchstone to our natures." With another metaphor he adds that Willoughby is not yet cured of "the passion of greed for the whole group of the well-favoured of the fair sex." The greed is, of course, incompatible with imaginative understanding. It would imprison the mind of another, not liberate Willoughby's own.

Though he has the still-adolescent devotion of Laetitia, who in her late twenties has been wooed by none, Willoughby accepts her adoration without feeling debtorship and pursues only the most popular girls. The comedy is in the incongruity of his expectation. He forgets that a young woman is popular because she has originality and spirit and that she must enjoy being in the main social current, else she would not attend balls and be eager to converse with men as well as women. Constantia exists for us in the novel just long enough to marry Harry Oxford and trip back into the world from which Willoughby as her fiancé would pluck her. Her escape establishes the character and the wound of the baronet when the eighteen-year-old Clara appears. Willoughby refuses to analyze Constantia's rebuff, but what makes it so cutting is that in worldly goods and position and in what he believes are gentlemanly accomplishments he is certainly superior to Oxford; it is his negative qualities which he dares not explore. Laetitia is a comfort in that he can afford not to marry her. He admits later that at times he needs "a Laetitia Dale to bring me out, give and take," but ironically in the light of what happens, he underlines, "*I could not marry Laetitia Dale.*" He will bestow her instead on "old Vernon" and keep her devotion to himself.

It has cost Willoughby nothing to find Laetitia already in his harem; the pleasure will be in bringing a younger and more beautiful inmate to take precedence over her. For once he has entrapped the inexperienced Clara the egoist makes deadly clear his expectation that she is to renounce the world. He pictures the satisfaction he will have when he is greeted by her on his return from hunting; she replies, "I am to be always at home?" He condescendingly assumes that there will be minor differences of opinion; she silently imagines him when they shall disagree. He likes the thought of a wife's remaining faithful to the memory of a dead husband; she has not yet brought herself to shut out the world for a living one. With all this he tells her an apt anecdote about male egoism and warns her never to marry an egoist. Now, one of Meredith's cardinal principles, revealed in his letters as well as in his fiction, was that marriage must represent not a retreat from the world but the addition of a comrade in the world's adventure. In Willoughby he was depicting what he regarded as one of the major sins of sentimentality in the Victorian age—a reversion to cave-man sentiments of possession and anti-intellectualism. The substance of his novel is a contest for liberation of a young mind eager to grow in enjoyment of adventure with an old mind which is nursing its wounds and trying desperately to hold its possessions. Without pushing the symbolism we can still find a contrast between Meredith's ideal in Clara of a marital condition to be and the old age in Willoughby of an outworn system of social mores and habits of thought.

Significantly in the contests between the baronet and the three women no masculine liberator is needed for any of the three. Constantia has voluntarily deserted after going to school to Willoughby. It is the egoist himself who unknowingly frightens Clara with the secrets of the harem: "Miss Middleton owed it to Sir Willoughby Patterne that she ceased to think like a girl." Clara does once try to find what Vernon would think if she jilted Willoughby, but she cannot so state the question as to get help because she does not want Vernon to admit toleration of jilting. She must by her own perceptions free herself and still not sacrifice her intense conviction that she has no right to injure Willoughby merely from self-concern. On the level of plot motif Meredith seized upon the not-too-obscure symbolism of the willow pattern in porcelain, which tells in pictures how a Chinese girl escapes both her tyrant father and a tyrant would-be husband to flee with her lover.[19] This is essentially what Clara does; and it is the type of girl on the china that the novelist has in mind when at the beginning Mrs. Mountstuart calls Clara a "dainty rogue in porcelain" and when Willoughby rejoices that there is "nothing of rogue" in himself. The vase was actually English; its story was for Meredith quite as pertinently English as Chinese. What is especially important in his novel and indeed basic to his theme is that, although Harry and Vernon are excellent companions to join, the dainty rogues have through their own skill freed themselves.

Though the author used no motif to represent the path by which Laetitia voluntarily enters the tyrant's castle after laying down her own conditions by ruthlessly calling Willoughby an egoist before him and his aunts, he made quite clear the fact that, like Constantia and Clara, Laetitia has gone to school to the baronet and has learned from experience the need for spiritual freedom. It is after his ambiguous friendship-love talk has tricked her into responding as a lover that she writes in her diary, "This day I was a fool. To-morrow?" Through such frank self-appraisal, which she naturally dreads but realistically applies, Laetitia eventually matures without losing entirely that subtle, wistful charm which has caused Mrs. Mountstuart to speak of the "romantic tale on her eyelashes."

Though Clara comes to love Vernon, the deepest affinity

and power of communion is actually between Clara and Laetitia. It is really the contrast betwen Willoughby's impercipience, echoed by that of Dr. Middleton and silently accepted by Mr. Dale, and the exquisite sensitivity of imagination of Clara and Laetitia that raises the novel to its highest interest. In this contrast we see the comedy of egoistic oblivion and the poignant charm of imaginative insight. Of examples of the egoist's blindness to the thoughts and feelings of others, a blindness which leaves him isolated and foolish, there is no end. A notable instance occurs upon his meeting Laetitia with the children after he has returned from his world tour to forget Constantia. He has looked into her eyes, and according to the author, "he found the man he sought there, squeezed him passionately, and let her go." He has no problem in wooing, for he has a stereotyped picture of a doll-like, ornamental wife. With Dr. Middleton, he can speak of women's whims, and each time Clara tries to talk seriously with him he crudely forces her back into his pattern.

In contrast are the minds of Laetitia and Clara, both of whom think of friendship and love as the going out of oneself into the mind of another. With Willoughby they are unsuccessful because the mind which they imagine for him is not equalled by the actual. In the whirlwind courtship Clara has had no inclination to judge, but as soon as she has been captured she begins to notice the minute incidental cruelties and acts of callousness which are symptomatic of major defects of mind and character. The anguish of her desperate attempt to build Willoughby nevertheless into her ideal, lest her whole world of ideals collapse, and her final triumph over the need to do so constitute her education. In developing to the utmost her kindness, her intelligence, and finally her courage, that education is Meredith's comic counterpart of the instruction in tragic sorrow of which De Quincey in "Levana and Our Ladies of Sorrow" was thinking when he let man's tutelary goddesses state their commission "to plague his heart until we had unfolded the capacities of his spirit."

Meredith has been accused of not completely championing the liberation of women because he regularly married his heroines instead of letting them have independent careers. For certain of his women marriage is the lesser evil and they accept it sacrificially. For them, including Laetitia, the novelist has pity. But as true marriage in Meredith's view was an expansion of one's imaginative horizons, he made such a union the fulfilment of a woman's life. When Clara imagines a husband she thinks of intellectual companionship, of the immersing oneself in human experience. This, the antithesis of desire for possession, means the losing of all feeling of isolation and the living within one mind the lives of two. It is not restrictive, as Meredith would not have either a man or a woman to shut out other lives upon marriage. His liberation of woman, really as much a liberation of man, involves not sending a woman along a path of unmarried friendship, but the redefining of marriage to give her all the freedom she would otherwise possess and in addition the special affinity of thought and feeling which union implies.

It is no Galahad that Clara wants for a husband. Indeed had she been in the pavilion when that hero passed triumphant from the lists adored by his harem, Clara would scarcely have interrupted her conversation with the witty courtier or court poet or gallant young page who happened to be beside her. But she has an ideal of husband none the less, and the strength of her spirit is tested in part by the blows which she sustains from Sir Willoughby before she renounces him as an utter contradiction to it. After several shocks she feels lonely and desperate, but she exerts her imagination once again to try to reconcile the ideal and actual, to find somewhere in the man a touch of the heroic. "But a solitary soul dragging a log," Meredith choruses, "must make the log a God to rejoice in the burden. That is not love." Torn between hope that she will find a god and a yearning for honorable retreat, Clara listens to Willoughby's aunts, hoping to share their enthusiasm and to disbelieve what her intellect tells her must be true, but "five minutes of him undid the work." This is still early in the story, and Clara must endure much more. Her antagonism kills the illusion of compatibility; she can no longer construct the egoist into an ideal. But her imagination still sustains an illusion when, having renounced love, she yields to pity. That Willoughby may suffer a blow to his *amour-propre* if she jilts him gives a new impulse and a new direction to her actions. She must find him a good wife and spare him shame; for though bitter from his treatment of her and of Laetitia, Clara can put herself in Willoughby's place as he cannot put himself in hers. Nothing short of her discovery that he has been dishonest in offering his hand to Laetitia and hypocritically denying the deed finally exempts her from pitying. As the wife of Vernon, in contrast, she will need neither pity nor delusion.

Clara's mind is the more fully revealed, but Laetitia's is not less subtle. Indeed the scenes in which they talk together are studies in the reverence of one mind for the sacredness of another. Two instances will illustrate. In the first Clara has perceived the egoist's cruelty to Laetitia and she feels that she must let her know that she has compassion for her. She begins by asserting that she would like being a coquette to capture "those lofty birds, the hawks" and punish them. Suddenly she becomes more pointed, but still indirect:

> "Here is the difference I see; I see it; I am certain of it: women who are called coquettes make their conquests not of the best of men; but men who are Egoists have *good* women for their victims; women on whose devoted constancy they feed; they drink it like blood. I am sure I am not taking the merely feminine view. They punish themselves too by passing over the one suitable to them, who could really give them what they crave to have, and they

> go where they . . ." [*sic.*] Clara stopped. "I have not your power to express ideas," she said.
>
> "Miss Middleton, you have a dreadful power," said Laetitia.

The other scene follows the midnight comedy of errors. Willoughby's tyranny over Crossjay, the locking him from his room, has caused the boy to hear the baronet's proposal to Laetitia and her reply. For Laetitia's ultimate good Clara must tell her that the story is abroad, but she gives a playful touch to her narrative:

> ". . . and he ran down to the drawing-room and curled himself up on the ottoman, and fell asleep, under that padded silken coverlet of the ladies—boots and all, I am afraid!"
>
> Laetitia profited by this absurd allusion, thanking Clara in her heart for the refuge.
>
> "He should have taken off his boots," she said.

It is their sense of the comic that makes possible this perfect communion of two spirits. In wedding Vernon, Clara will continue to enjoy an attunement of minds; but unless Clara revisits Laetitia, the new lady of Patterne Hall will know such affinity only in retrospect.

Imagination and truth must eventually triumph; otherwise Meredith's faith would be unfulfilled. Clara escapes back to the world, and Laetitia, though her life will remain pathetic, casts off the spell of enchantment, the romantic idolization of a sultan, and is ready to add Willoughby to her sphere without giving up all her newly found freedom for him. And the egoist himself must be somewhat more honest at the end; if not there would be no value in thwackings. In the metaphor of *The Shaving of Shagpat* he may be said to have caught a strong whiff of the gall of the Roc. Mrs. Mountstuart quite frankly marks for him the desperate stage he has reached: "You show your under-teeth too at times when you draw in a breath, like a condemned highcaste Hindoo my husband took me to see in a jail in Calcutta, to give me some excitement when I was pining for England." When he hopes that he has salvaged a little of his reputation, that he can pretend to rejoice in being rid of Clara, his bitterness suddenly turns to its worst:

> He had won a desperate battle, but what had he won? . . . Just a shirt, it might be said. . . . Lady Busshe was unbearable. . . . And Mrs. Mountstuart was hardly much above her. . . . And for what [had he sacrificed]? . . . For the favourable looks and tongues of these women whose looks and tongues he detested!

Willoughby, unlike Shibli, has been unable to pluck the hair from the horse Garaveen, that is, to capture enthusiasm. His actions are inspired by fear and their reward is ashes and grit. He cannot sever the Identical because he cannot manage the Sword of Aklis, the magical instrument of imagination. Yet he is not a complete victim of the Roc and, despite the determination of Mrs. Mountstuart and Lady Busshe, he will not return to the Hall of Asses. Certainly he has had no luck in the Hall of Maidens. The imagination of others cannot engraft in his mind enthusiasms and insight which would find no nourishment there. But it has trimmed his beard and forced him to look at his naked face in a mirror—a mirror which does not magnify and glamorize his leg.

The theme of the novel is itself engaging. On it Meredith evolved an ingenious plot with variations on the main idea. Willoughby has an occasional slight triumph only to discover its hollowness; like the Countess de Saldar, he is a general, though mainly he must glorify petty victory and rationalize heavy defeat. Suspense steadily builds up as he sacrifices first one, then another standard of decorum in the increasingly desperate gamble to win or at least not to lose too much. Finally comes his overthrow, which because of his egoism was inevitable from the beginning, but which still comes as a sudden reversal, catching him by surprise. For Meredith the working out of the general pattern was perhaps no great challenge. In *The Shaving of Shagpat* once he had established his values he could improvise without fear of straying, and in *The Egoist* he could likewise explore whatever was within his province without losing his direction. The interest was therefore not alone in seeing the main theme and making the reader see it, but also in pursuing for short distances the innumerable variations and then discovering their kinship. The consequence is that one perceives both the variety and the unifying pattern.

Important in the variety is the spirit of fun, which refuses to be held to any one type of comedy. There are Terentian intrigue, Molière hypocrisy, Peacockian fantasy, Congrevean battle of wits, and Shakespearean clowning. Like Terence's young rake, Willoughby starts irresponsibly by violating Laetitia's sensibility and ends by marrying her. He is at times, and especially near the close, as hypocritical as Tartuffe in his accusing Clara of disloyalty after he has proposed marriage to Laetitia and been rejected. In what Willoughby would regard as a proper, dignified manner he performs an Andrew Aguecheek caper to win Clara's attention; the resemblance is unmistakable and the effect equally ludicrous. The night scene is a comedy of errors; it is followed by another mad one in which no one understands anyone else. There is comparable farce in the dialogue of the two aunts, who think so exactly alike that one ends the other's sentences. More Peacockian in substance and method are the bacchanal scenes in which the Machiavellian Willoughby serves Dr. Middleton his choicest wines. The doctor too has been unlucky with women, in fact, with both wife and child:

> Her mother had been an amiable woman, of the poetical temperament nevertheless, too enthusiastic, imaginative, impulsive, for the repose of a sober scholar; an admirable

> woman, still, as you see, a woman, a firework. The girl resembled her.

Now, under his host's machinations the sober scholar expands warmly and generously: "A fresh decanter was placed before the doctor. He said: 'I have but a girl to give'." A daughter is not an extravagant price for the affluence of the Patterne cellar.

While pursuing the ramifications of egoism, hypocrisy, mental sterility, and comic sensuality Meredith also employed images and symbols to suggest unity of design. Some we have already noticed. Mrs. Mountstuart's label of Constantia as a "racing cutter," of Clara as a "dainty rogue in porcelain," of Vernon as "Phoebus Apollo turned fasting friar," her reference to the romantic tale on Laetitia's eyelashes and to Willoughby's leg—all these remind us that the characters are not unique, but typical of generic values. The name Patterne is indicative. The vase motif, including both the veiled allusion to the willow pattern and the breaking of De Craye's wedding gift, which at least anticipates the breaking of the engagement, is arbitrarily imposed, but its analogy directs our attention toward the theme. Clara speaks of the dog star and Dr. Middleton is puzzled because it is associated with Agamemnon's sacrifice of his daughter; we perceive, of course, the novelist's stress on the epic antiquity of his theme. References to the Book of Egoism also turn us back from the particular to the universal, as do the frisking of the comic imps and the smiling of the Comic Muse herself. Scattered through six-hundred pages, these allusions are not obtrusive. They are just sufficiently apparent to remind us that underlying the action of the novel is a design comparable to that in the allegory on Shagpat and that, while keeping to his moral purpose of correcting society through the use of comedy, Meredith has retained the artist's delight in the creative work for its own sake as an adventure of the imagination.

Chapter Five

Romance as a Vision of Truth

They have no song, the sedges dry,
And still they sing.
It is within my breast they sing,
As I pass by.
Within my breast they touch a string,
They wake a sigh.
There is but sound of sedges dry;
In me they sing.
(Song in the Songless)

In his essay "Wordsworth in the Tropics," 1929, Mr. Aldous Huxley rebukes both Wordsworth and Meredith for their naïveté. Nature in the torrid zones, he maintains, is actually a ruthless destroyer of men, in no sense the docile slave which they seemed to find at latitude fifty:

> The life of those vast masses of swarming vegetation is alien to the human spirit and hostile to it. Meredith, in his "Woods of Westermain," has tried reassuringly to persuade us that our terrors are unnecessary, that the hostility of these vegetable forces is more apparent than real, and that if we will but trust Nature, we shall find our fears transformed into serenity, joy, and rapture. This may be sound

> philosophy in the neighborhood of Dorking; but it begins to be dubious even in the forests of Germany. . . .

In the "Woods of Westermain" the poet was using the forest to symbolize a sensitive, romantic life, though what he says may still be tested against Huxley's specific, literal meaning of *woods,* since the influence of nature upon him is part of the condition of man's life. Meredith's concept of man's relation to nature is rather different, however, from the view credited to him by Huxley.

Meredith—and I believe Wordsworth—would have granted their critic the fact that in the tropics vegetation grows with such violence and the rains may come in such torrents that a man trying to clear an acre of land or otherwise to maintain a civilized self-discipline is in danger of both physical and spiritual defeat. Moreover, although the poets are blamed for confining their impressions to the temperate climates, one suspects that both would be more realistic than their accuser. They would admit that the difference between the latitudes was in degree rather than in kind and that it was perhaps less real than apparent. But there would remain a fundamental difference between the perspectives of Huxley and Meredith. For the essayist the sedges, whether drenched with tropical deluges or dry with English August heat, do not sing; and to pretend that they do is to have an illusion that nature is a comforting protector in which man can trust. Meredith is, for Huxley, guilty of such an illusion. Actually, as the poet makes clear, whatever singing occurs is within man's heart. The phenomena of the natural world "touch a string," but whether the response will be one of exuberant joy, pensive sadness, or despair is dependent on the heart, not on the phenomena alone. The touching of the string may be gentle or pronounced, but the strength and sensitivity of the human spirit determine the harmony or discord which results. It is not weak spirits, Meredith tells us, who are to venture far into the magical woods; these will be lost in a wilderness, in Huxley's tropics, we could say. But for the intellectually courageous and imaginative the woods provide awe rather than craven fear, and if we may transpose Chaucer's words, they are "the wey to al good aventure."

Romance was for Meredith not a quality to be attained by any set pattern of philosophic thought; as in Wordsworth's poem, it came like a phantom "to haunt, to startle, and waylay." Yet, as to Wordsworth, it would come with lasting frequency only to the sternly disciplined imagination. The essential function of brain in the trinity—blood, brain, spirit—was to discriminate amid the great welter of experience and to exclude and select. When the mind could imagine beauty and hold the image long enough to free it of all that was unbeautiful, it achieved one of its highest functions. Meredith did not assume that life was at all times a romance, or even that it was often preoccupied intensely with the beautiful. But as a poet and novelist he was concerned with exclusion and selection. There is herein no conflict with the recognition of actuality as in some respects a tropical wilderness. Nor is there an assumption that the mind is independent of the external world. For Meredith a blue sky or a fresh spring shower or a mountain vista did affect man's imagination. But whether the result was merely a pleasant momentary joy stemming from the senses and dying formlessly or whether it found orderly identification in the mind was dependent on the mind's capacity for artistic synthesis.

Even as we find comedy in nearly every story which Meredith wrote though most strikingly in a few, so romance waylays us again and again in both prose and poems. To select, therefore, is only to suggest the ubiquity of its presence.

For our purposes *Love in the Valley* is important because it presented a series of lyric scenes which anticipated in spirit the tone of similar scenes in the novels. First printed in 1851, when Meredith was twenty-three years old, the poem was republished in 1878 with no essential change in tone. Long after 1878, in fact, Meredith could still recapture the zest for beauty and the joy in nature and in love which surcharged both versions of the poem.

The valley is idyllic and the girl is an idealization. They are no more of England, except for incidental scenery and customs than of the tropics, but belong rather to the tradition of idylls and Arcady. Yet they have not only a consistency within themselves—a quality which alone would not make them either true or real—but resemblances to things within our mental experience, and so we can translate them, even as we can Shibli's adventures, into actual life. All that the poet has done has been to give in pure form a charm and beauty which are ordinarily known imperfectly because they are obscured by distracting, discordant elements.

In the poem the beauty of nature is represented in tangible things—the colors of the dogwood and whitebeam, the wildflowers, the shadow prints of trees, and the fresh contrasts of sunshine and dewy morning and eve. The scenes are aesthetically pleasing as individual studies in color and motion. They are, in addition, suggestive of a cosmic order which offers such beauty in profusion for him who can perceive it. They are the more profound poetically in that they are apprehended by the complete mind, not alone by that faculty by which one abstracts generalizations. They startle the imagination into a new awareness, till it begins to doubt its habitual, complacent acceptance of nature and to venture into a new world. One may refuse to accept them as anything except illusions if one is convinced that the phenomena of our world represent a lawless riot of mad "tropical" meaninglessness. But for Meredith himself there was no question of illusion; he was immediately entranced with scenes which, with the full support of his senses, his imagination represented as ethereally beautiful and real.

The girl, seen through the lover's eyes, is essentially like the lyre which Shelley wished to become and also like his maiden in "The Sensitive Plant." Her attunement to birds' songs, her communion with flowers, both the wild ones and the "prim little scholars" of her garden, her anticipation of the moods of weather, her "wild" grace of motion—all represent the human epitome of what the lover finds excellent in nature. Gossips may talk of his beloved as of a creature of earth, with imperfections of feature, "beauty not complete," but the lover rejoins:

> . . . beauty that makes holy
> Earth and air, may have faults from head to feet.

The lover's affinity with his beloved is in the romantic tradition. He does not know nor does he seek to learn the complete nature of her personality. The things which he chooses to contemplate are those that symbolize beauty. His love represents a freeing of his own mind from concern for self, and an unceasingly fresh adventure. It is not an irresponsible riot of emotion; rather it is a severely disciplined experience in which nothing is permitted to detract from what the poet finds dear. In the poem there are no comic contrasts, because the lover does not stray from his ideal and need to be brought back to it. There is no hint of tragedy because there is no sensation of mortality. The poem differs from most pastorals and even from such a romantic love poem as *The Eve of St. Agnes* in that there are no harsh contrasts for emphasis. Despite its many incidents, it describes one single emotion of joy. In the novels the emotion was to reappear, but as part of a manifold pattern, with comedy or tragedy or both.

In *The Shaving of Shagpat* the resemblance of the romantic tone to that of *The Arabian Nights* is immediately apparent. Though the adventures of Shibli are held in order by a comic perspective and those of Bhanavar by a tragic one, there is delight in the separate incidents themselves as expressions of an imaginative quest. Meredith stresses the enthusiasm which keeps Shibli determined to attain his goal. The lad plunges courageously into an adventure, discovers that he has been on the pathway of error, reverses his direction, and renews the search, only to dash once more into folly and again, after a thwacking, to start anew to master the event. His life is full of error; in one sense anything which does not lead him toward his ideal is error. But his constant resurgence of enthusiasm and his concept of the Event as the unifying touchstone of experience bespeak a quality in man's mind that is not entirely destroyed even by his recognition of his endless folly. It is not courage alone which drives him; it is imagination. Shibli sees a future condition so intensely that he lives in and for it. It may be in part illusory, and the bright light of intellect may be needed to dispel the illusion. But it is, however obscurely, related to the ideal itself, as it is through the pursuit of imperfect forms and the wisdom he learns therefrom that he comes nearer to the ideal.

In fact, romantic adventure always involved for Meredith both an ideal, even if vaguely perceived by the hero, and enthusiasm. As he reveals in Wilfrid Pole, the casual enthusiast with no steadfast devotion may mount Hippogriff and for a while be a better man than before; but his enthusiasm soon wanes, and having strayed onto a byroad he dismounts and deplores his ill luck instead of returning at full gallop for a fresh start. Though the complete romantic, on the other hand, may not be able to tell what it is that he is seeking, the ideal glimpses that come into his imagination save him from corruption and make him sensitive to goodness and beauty. Needless to say, Meredith's grown men, except for here and there a character introduced as a norm, are but imperfectly romantic. Humanly fallible, the best of them are susceptible to distractions which misdirect their enthusiasm. Their comedy is in the earnestness with which they wander about, the romance in their attunement to ideals.

Transitional between the allegory and the more realistic novels, though still very close to the former, is *Farina,* published in 1856. Its main subject matter is chivalric adventures and love of a gallant lad, Farina, for a rose-lipped damsel. By way of contrast is the supernatural contest of a monk with Satan. Light in tone, the story opens with the atmosphere of the vine-covered hills of the Rhineland, and it concludes with a reference to the vines. Margarita is a worthy merchant's daughter, who loves the legendary Siegfried and weaves his history into a tapestry; Farina is a poor youth unworthy of being a member of the "White Rose Club," an organization dedicated to duelling in Margarita's honor. The lovers' adventures are playfully but affectionately described, with the help of Rhineland legends and Minnesinger and nightingale songs, and with the accompaniment of supernatural incidents —the transformation of a lily into the Lady of the Water and the terrifying fall of Satan from the Drachenstein into Cologne amid thunder and lightning.

Margarita is a very sensible lass despite her sheltered existence. She discovers that the Siegfried of her tapestry is remarkably like Farina and no transfer of affection is needed. Later, when her hero is rescuing her, she is skillful in handling a weapon to assist. She will make a good burgher's wife. Farina, in contrast, until the mastery of his Event is an impulsive, impractical, reckless lad, who lives exclusively in his love for the White Rose and in the excitement of the adventures which his love brings. His companion, the Goshawk, chivalrous and idealistic, yet heartily robust and practical, is the touchstone by which Farina is to be judged. And Monk Gregory is a symbol of a less rewarding kind of quest, which in its stress on spirit pays scant attention to brain and denies the relevance of blood.

When Farina sees the moon he calls it a goddess, and the

Goshawk "wistfully" assents. In words anticipating the love scenes of *The Ordeal of Richard Feverel* and of *Lord Ormont and His Aminta* Meredith characterizes the lover:

> The soul of a lover lives through every member of him in the joy of a moonlight ride. . . . He must strike all the strings of life. Swiftness is his rapture. In his wide arms he embraces the whole form of beauty.

The hero's faith is rewarded when the Lady of the Water, appearing first as a water lily in the moonlight, guides him to the rescue of his beloved. In contrast to Farina is the monk. As the two ride together Farina is in a "silver-fleeting glory"; his companion is "as a shadow." The adversary whom Farina fights is a bold robber baron, wicked to a point, yet sufficiently honorable to abide by the rules of swordplay. The youth, in short, faces obstacles of circumstance rather than a struggle of conscience. But Satan is a much more cunning foe. Like a typical sentimentalist he uses the odor of a lily to counteract his natural brimstone stench. What is worst about him is his base treachery. He lets Gregory subdue him on the cliff, but he still delivers a "back blow." Gregory has conquered all evils, including the supreme one of pride, and so in the exultation upon his conquest he glories. An honest man, he discovers his sin: ". . . vanity has wrecked me. . . . He gave me easy victory to inflate me." It is indicative that, with all his self-castigation, the monk cannot chase Satan from Cologne. Not until Farina returns does the archfiend yield. It is the wholesome outward-looking of romance that rids the city of his spell.

With sharp comedy, however, Meredith traces the decline of the romantic youth from the moonlight of fairy water nymphs into the common day of mercantile burghers. To tell us that Farina prospered he remarks that Satan repeated his back blow. And when the Goshawk later visits the now successful and esteemed middle-class citizen, he is "waylaid by false Farinas." The singleness of heart and the indifference to worldly success have given way to mundane considerations, and it is not until the Goshawk finds him alone with his family that the true Farina appears.

In *The Ordeal of Richard Feverel,* 1859, there are so many diverse elements that their relationship demands a separate chapter. The romantic parts are not fully separable from the tragedy since the Saturnine influence of Sir Austin is upon them, but there are moments when Richard, forgetting his father and himself, lives intensely in adventure. The burning of Farmer Blaize's rick and the reading of Latude's escapes to plot the rescue of Tom Bakewell from jail suggest a daring spirit; and the courage with which Richard, even in his pride, determines to play the hero by sacrificing himself to save Tom is the quality of a hero of romance.

From dreaming on the prettiness of girls' names and writing verses about his cousin Clare, Richard is suddenly awakened in an earthly paradise. Knowing nothing of his father's Great Shaddock Dogma, which assumes that Eve invariably eats of the apple and persuades Adam to eat, he is in Eden before the coming of the serpent. With an ideal concept of courtly love, he finds Lucy on the bank of a pastoral stream, and the ideal instantly, as for Margarita, becomes real. The two are Ferdinand and Miranda blissfully without knowledge that the guardian of their fates is no wise Prospero. For Richard, and presumably for Lucy, all earth is transformed. He lives in two worlds at once, or rather, he moves from habit through the old one and lives in the new, which, despite its strangeness, its precarious fragility, alone seems real. That this world shall be destroyed through the machinations of the would-be magician and the folly of Richard himself is only evidence that human life is tragically mortal, that the mind is subject to the relentless badgering of time. But for a little while Richard has lived where time does not exist. The contrast becomes the sharper when he has shut the gates on his earthly Eden and then clamors vainly for readmittance.

In its range *Evan Harrington* is much more circumscribed than *The Ordeal.* There is no tragedy, of course, for the hero, and the pathos in the novel arises from the loneliness, the private sorrows, of the minor women characters; its pertinence for Evan is that it brings a melancholy seriousness into what would otherwise be a shallow life. Evan himself is in circumstance an English Farina, who as a tailor's son has no right to be a member of any White Rose club; and Rose Jocelyn is much like Margarita, her Siegfried being Evan Harrington gentleman, untainted by trade and enveloped in the aura of embassies. Less reckless than Farina, Evan has heroism thrust upon him. He sees no supernatural ladies, knows no courtly love songs, is not enthralled by the notes of nightingales. He is, in fact, a most ordinary youth in love with a high-spirited, but unformed and essentially uneducated girl. Besides, he is at times incapable of positive action because the gentleman who is loved cannot acknowledge the tailor who loves. Yet, with all his comic confusion, Evan is always in or wandering close to the very heart of romance.

The Rose he loves has so little understanding of her indebtedness to society that Evan must tell her in elementary fashion the relation of plebeian trade and glamorous ships. In bravado she risks his neck in an unnecessary race. She goes boldly and independently about her pleasure seeking, with no thought of the desperate turmoil in the hearts of others. She has indeed very glaring "faults from head to feet." Yet the image of her in Evan's mind is the talisman which most raises his life above drab desolation; without it he would truly be but the ninth part of a man. The Countess de Saldar must live in an aristocratic world to clothe herself in illusion of her own importance; but Evan, though by nature he prefers embassy to shop, values the aristocratic atmosphere around Rose primarily because she is its center.

What Rose finds in Evan is equally limited. She has never seen him in action; the race is a substitute test because she does not know the true ordeal which he is undergoing. He is to her a rather handsome, well-mannered youth who is fond of her. The romance has as its theme the increase in stature of both lovers, a growth which comes from the love itself. As Rose learns who it really is that loves her she develops understanding; and when he knows his beloved sufficiently to have faith in her, Evan can admit with pride his true nature. These are not mature lovers—a Weyburn and Aminta, an Owain Wythan and Carinthia; they are adolescents impelled very strongly by blood. But they develop a wholesome adequacy of brain, so that their betrothal in the shop announces the fact that at last Rose has identified her Siegfried with her real knight and that Evan has for wife a person of much more wisdom and sympathy than the young girl whose nature, though he loved her devotedly, he could not trust.

As the novel is a comedy and Meredith does not wish to sentimentalize by making his characters infallible, we must predict for Evan and Rose a future comparable to that of Farina and Margarita. The marriage will prosper and Satan may manage a back blow. Certainly in the middle-aged husband and successful citizen a visiting Goshawk—Jack Raikes is not a sufficient proxy—might have some difficulty in finding the true Evan. But that is only to say that even for lovers time will not forever stand still.

When Meredith wrote *Emilia in England* (later renamed *Sandra Belloni*), published in 1864, he was still experimenting freely, and the result was a mélange of tragedy, comedy, and romance. One of the best studies in the novel is of the pathetic aging of old Pole, and others concern the comic or tragicomic lives of the Pole children and Purcell Barrett. Yet he named the book for his heroine and stated that she was a "touchstone" by which the Pole family could be judged. His portrait of her is only moderately successful, and it appears that Meredith himself was still unsure about it at the end; he was trying to embody an ideal in a real woman and to give her much more complexity of nature than he had given Rose Jocelyn and Lucy Feverel.

He stressed Emilia's practical nature—her ability to subsist on potatoes and to care for her impoverished family, to nurse Pole, to live diplomatically amidst falseness and suspicion. He contrasted her sincerity and courage as a lover with Wilfrid's vacillation. But above all he emphasized her intense enjoyment of music, her devotion to Italian freedom, and her enthusiastic acceptance of life as a thrilling adventure. She may suffer acutely, but whereas the others venture timidly and evade decisions, she is almost wholly immune to self-consciousness. She is, in fact, an embodiment of a faith in life which Meredith, as well as Matthew Arnold, found but seldom in Victorian England.

Since the novelist could not reproduce the music of his heroine's singing, he had to resort to enveloping her in an atmosphere appropriate to the mood of her song and to dramatize its effect. Before Emilia herself appears her voice is heard floating through the night air of the countryside, and the Poles find her alone, indifferent to danger or decorum, singing as unrestrainedly as a nightingale. Later, in the tent of the country merry-makers, who still keep up once a year the traditions of "old England," she, as a foreigner to the scene, soon becomes the lyric expression of the rustic vigor and robust exuberance which Meredith never ceased to idealize. Each time she sings it is as if, recalling Keats' "Ode on a Grecian Urn," the novelist delighted in making word pictures convey the beauty of music. The supreme example was to come in the sequel, *Vittoria,* 1867, where he first built up the tense atmosphere in the Milan theater, with patriots waiting eagerly and Austrians anxiously as they listened to a transparent operatic allegory on tyranny. When the tension is near a climax it is Vittoria, that is, Emilia, who sings the ringing words, "Italia, Italia shall be free." Only song, Meredith believed, could adequately express the spirit of Italian passion for freedom, and in both novels the heroine prizes her gift because song is the direct, untrammeled manifestation of spiritual liberty and therefore of her devotion to the Italian cause.

But Meredith would also have Emilia live in the light of common day. Her improvident father has a skill in music which inspires her to say that his playing can make one feel oneself from head to toe, that it is like a "thread of honey drawn through your heart." But he is unscrupulous and parasitic. Emilia has enjoyed the beauty and has accepted the poverty, but she has been repelled by the base proposals to which her father has wanted her to listen. She wishes to love devotedly, but mistakenly cherishes Wilfrid, who cannot appreciate her genius. Her loyalty to Italy while she is yet in England is not sufficient expression of her feminine nature. Despite early hardships she is not a mature woman. Nursing old Pole, whom she pities, gives her a feminine role, but significantly it is temporary loss of her power to sing that rescues her from the peril of Amazonian megalomania. Without her talent she must discover the rest of her nature, hitherto only partially revealed. She becomes interested in clothing, in being pretty, in being helped. Then, when she has cured herself of her illusion about Wilfrid, she is ready to go to Italy, and with assurance that she will go the novel ends. The theme of Emilia's history is the humanizing of a spirit that it may start anew on its mission stronger and more understanding than before.

As one recalls the incidents of the novel one is struck with the extent to which it is about others than Emilia herself. In the welter of circumstance she plays only the role which in actual society she might be expected to have as one of many persons, each living intensely, even desperately, and at times in mental isolation. Meredith could not exclude incidents merely because they did not influence Emilia's own life. Despite his title he was concerned with society as an orchestra, with solo parts but with each instrument also having its peculiar function in the ensemble. Romance as represented by Emilia and by the adventures in which she participates furnished for the novelist the unifying strain. Once introduced, it is always present in the reader's mind, even when it exists in memory or in anticipation.

In *Vittoria,* 1867, the full significance of the romantic perspective becomes apparent only when one recognizes how many otherwise chaotic incidents the focus has brought into order. *Vittoria* is just sufficiently the sequel to *Sandra Belloni* for the continuity to be disturbing. Having resolved the heroine's conflicts in the first novel, Meredith had to make her again somewhat immature, though much less so than before, so that she could again develop in character as a romantic heroine. Consequently, in turning from *Sandra Belloni* to the sequel the reader retains a ghost image of Sandra in many ways incompatible with the new portrait. Yet unless one has read the earlier work, he can not fully understand some of Vittoria's actions. The heroine, now christened by the Italian patriots "Vittoria Campa," is both an exalted feminine embodiment of the spirit of freedom and a person capable of trying, as the other Italians do, to protect her friends on the Austrian side, and so of being confused in her mind and of being regarded as a liability by other patriots. Again Meredith wanted to do so much that his canvas teemed with characters—one hundred and nine have been counted—and with incidents exemplifying heroism and friendship and double dealing, suspicion, and cowardice; devotion to country and sabotage of the cause through devotion to family; adoration of women and refusal to give them any voice in counsel; routine daily living and melodramatic adventure. The novel was meant to give a panoramic sketch of Italy in its struggle—a revolution in which folly and baseness were prominent and from which no immediate gain was to come, yet a struggle which strengthened nobility of character and which was the only way toward eventual liberation.

As in *Sandra Belloni,* Vittoria is usually off the stage; but, often arbitrarily, to be sure, her actions provide a loose continuity and her experience frequently recapitulates that of others. Pledged to the cause of liberty, she admires the genius of the "Chief," the unnamed Mazzini, a power felt in the background; she pities and respects King Carlo Alberto, suspected and opposed by the chief's followers; she befriends Austrians and their English sympathizers, including Wilfrid; once to rescue an Italian she insincerely draws on Wilfrid's mild affection for her; and, like an Italian girl who has loved an Austrian, she finds herself once admiring a handsome Austrian officer, whose bearing reminds her of Carlo Ammiani, her lover and later her husband. She attempts, as do other women, to give sensible advice, only to be ignored. Besides having many unexpected adventures—imprisonment, flight, intrigue—she welcomes danger and hard toil by becoming a nurse within earshot of the guns. Like others, she is made a widow.

In spite of the arbitrary knitting together of the multiple themes—even the eccentric Pericles is involved in the plotting and the traffic with the enemy—the novel is convincing in its portrayal of honor and human dignity. Without this the intrigues would be commonplace or perhaps sordid. Whether it presents the haughty yet chivalric generosity of the Austrian Weisspriess, the quixotic march of Wilfrid with a white, that is, Austrian umbrella through the irate Italian mob, the dog-like faithfulness of Carlo's cousins, or Carlo's own courageous death, the story is never of man's defeat by physical suffering, but of the unconquerable determination of his spirit. The action of the novel seems to be mainly of the years 1848-1849. In 1866, during the renewal of the war against Austria and before the actual publication of *Vittoria,* Meredith visited Italy as a correspondent and learned at close range what he had previously had to imagine on the basis of his knowledge of human nature. Yet he did not choose to include any of the human degradation which later novelists were to associate with war. We may well feel that in entering the province of the journalist by taking as his subject an actual uprising Meredith should by no means have considered himself so free to select and exclude as in his other novels. If, on the other hand, we contrast him with his predecessors in the historical novel, we find that he has given a highly complex picture of what went on in the minds of his characters, that the anguish of thought has not been omitted from the report. In the conscious mind, which is Meredith's concern in *Vittoria,* romantic idealism has had to struggle with all the pressures that he can marshal against it, and in his interpretation it is triumphant.

Convinced that romance was valid, Meredith from the beginning attempted to distinguish it from pesudoromance and from sentimental egoism masking in its image. But he could not rest satisfied with a conviction until he had tested it against the strongest objections which good sense could supply. *The Adventures of Harry Richmond,* 1871, became his new proving ground.

Whatever was the origin of a belief in fairyland, the history of that belief shows one of man's eternal problems. In *Aucassin et Nicolette* the lovers have only two alternatives—to go to Heaven and boredom or to join the fine ladies and gentlemen in Hell. Elfland seems at times to have been an escape from both realms. In "Thomas Rymer" the road to Heaven is uninviting and that to Hell disastrous, but there is the "bonny" path which winds to elfland. Presumably fairyland was intended to be a place exempt from responsibilities, where moral obligation did not exist, where there was no conflict of ego and circumstance. Yet significantly in the same poem restrictions soon appear. One must wade through blood and, though the reasons are not those of earth, there are absolute taboos on conduct. Elsewhere in folklore elfland is sometimes a sinister place, either a limbo of those eternally separated from human feeling or a perversely evil land. It is, in fact, not easily possible for man to believe consistently in a bonny freedom from circumstance. Tennyson pictured the delights in the land of the lotus eaters, but he was already temperamentally committed to the theme of "Ulysses." The lure of *The Arabian Nights* for Meredith and the rest of us is perhaps that more than most other books it seems to provide a fairyland in which the mind can linger without the encroachment of our usual moral concern or worry about man's ordinary struggle against circumstance. It has its own moral order, and its heroes have no cause for qualms of conscience.

There were times in life, particularly in youth, Meredith believed, when absorption in adventure made existence a veritable Arabian Night romance. But there was always too the sober, gray world of duty with which one could not compromise. Though the novelist deplored Victorian puritanism, feeling that the puritans believed in a divine power hostile to human enjoyment, he did not ignore circumstance. *Harry Richmond* is his story of man's revolt against the trammels that would keep him earthbound. There was in everyone, Meredith was convinced, a longing to fly without wings, to take what one wanted of beauty and adventure without thought of payment. Were man not so driven he would be but a dull ox. Yet he could not fly and he must pay.

If the protagonist were merely an unimaginative egoist having the world's standard of values and determined to get someone else's share, the resolving of his conflict would involve only his seeing his right proportion within the world which he accepted. Meredith's theme is more inclusive, indeed of the kind often thought best for tragedy. When, as in *Vathek, The Travels of St. Leon,* and *Melmoth the Wanderer,* the hero transcends mortal limitations he loses moral touch with humanity and is tragic. Meredith, realizing that the yearning to escape from earthly considerations is not restricted to those who end tragically, sought without supernatural machinery to study the impulse to outleap man's mortal nature and the contrary circumstantial force that brings one back.

For the child Harry his grandfather Beltham, the country squire, represents stodgy, respectable security, the annihilation of romance; his father, Richmond Roy, all that is magnificently uninhibited and heroic. With the squire are associated Harry's sweet, docile aunt and his cousin Janet. In his father's camp is the school hero, Heriot, arrogant with ushers and imperious with Julia, who loves him. The life of the gipsies, which Harry sometimes shares, is a free, adventurous one separate from both the others; and Kiomi, as the epitome of its courage and virtue, is always for Harry a wholesome norm, indeed romance firmly supported by ethics.

Only when with Kiomi, and not always then, can the youthful Harry forget the war between the Beltham and Richmond Roy factions of his nature. As he grows into adolescence and early manhood the battle develops intensity. To placate conscience he pays his father's extravagant debts, without, however, considering that the money given him for the purpose represents someone's toil; and when the Roy star is ascendant he feels that living on an unrealistically magnificent scale is not wrong, that life should be an uninhibited assertion of the ego unthreatened by spiritual pain or death.

Ottilia as a German princess is like a fairy lady in his imagination, and without thought of whether he has worth to offer he acquiesces in his father's scheme to ensnare her. Presented in an atmosphere of high cultivation reminiscent of *Die Wahlverwandtschaften,* Ottilia seems to Harry to be of the air as intensely as Janet seems of earth. Indeed his glamorized picture of the life of the nobility and of royalty is his version of elfland. He would live in it an amoral existence, with no intrusion of the Beltham world of circumstance. In the comradeship of Heriot, in the continental tours with his father, and in his visit at the German palace, Harry experiences a divine intoxication of spirit. Yet, though he tries to transcend stern ethical circumstance by ignoring its unmistakable evidence, he is never really at peace. Over and over his lack of poise, of taste, and of security—the mark of his earth-bound nature—makes him turn to some new extravagance or other madcap act. Little by little, however, though with frequent lapses, the truth forces itself upon him. Heriot as a would-be seducer of the now married Julia is, he perceives, not only immoral but ungentlemanly. As Harry recalls his own life in Germany he has to compare himself unfavorably with the true gentlemen he met there. And he must admit that even after his father quit spending, he himself outdid Roy on a last fling of extravagance. To be sure, in telling his own history he does not pretend to have become a philosopher, for then he would be an intolerable prig. He merely tells what he did, but what he remembers shows not only the life he most loved, but also what imprinted itself upon his memory because it was a painful contradiction of his dream. Instead of being able to escape from the limitations of his ego he has had to admit their rigor and to recognize himself as a specific mortal being actually inferior to many others.

The supremely comic incident for Harry comes when the diablerie of Roy has brought Ottilia to his home in England and the Beltham forces have brought Janet there too. Harry, who could previously be in love simultaneously with Kiomi, Ottilia, a pretty country girl, and a slightly-known actress, is now wondering which of the two women to marry. Janet makes him "gasp for air," but Ottilia makes him "long for earth." But what remains in his mind is that when he met them together they were delighted in each other's company and utterly indifferent to his presence. Eventually Harry realizes that all the time Ottilia has been sensibly practical; it has been he alone who placed her in a fanciful, enchanted bower where he would come to release her. In fact, in refusing to wed Harry even when scandal threatened, she has been saner than Janet, who meanwhile has idealistically waited at the altar for a worthless rake whom she pitied and hoped to reform. In the first version Harry unjustly reproaches Janet and then introspectively examines his own passions before she marries him. Though the final version still leaves the courtship too scant, Meredith did improve the consistency by eliminating the sentimental outburst.[20] As the book now reads, Harry proposes and Janet unhesitantly accepts. Not able even now to perceive fully her imaginative nature, since she does not wear her heart conspicuously, Harry consoles himself with the thought that one cannot expect sentiment from a "Damascus blade."

The most cruel blow which he is made to suffer is seeing Beltham break Roy by exposing his fabulous pretensions and disclosing that Roy and Harry have been unknowingly living on the secret bounty of Harry's aunt. Perhaps his lowest spiritual descent is in his being ashamed of Roy not for wrong doing but for being ridiculous. Roy's pathetic resignation and heroic death, of which we shall speak elsewhere, reaffirm his faith and admiration.

As the story is really of a youth's education in romance Harry exists essentially as a consciousness madly striving for romance, distressed by whatever mundane restrictions say, "Thou canst not," and above all subtly impressionable. Through the incidents which record themselves on his consciousness we see that what he once held cheap as of the earth he comes to hold dear and that what he admired for its ethereal glamor he either rejects or accepts afresh on more valid grounds. In her sentimental devotion to Roy his aunt, he perceives, has had a romantic ideal without which her life would be colorless. In casting aside Heriot for the love of her husband, Julia has entered a delightful new world. Kiomi, Janet, and Ottilia have all through suffering achieved the independence of spirit which Harry once thought possible only for the one who lived romantically above the sorrows of the earth. Beltham has made such an ideal of integrity that morality itself is in him grandly heroic. As he becomes able to see these truths Harry also sees the magnificent Roy more clearly than before. It is not the glamor to which his father introduced him that he now values but the amazing resources of Roy's imagination and the pathos of his fruitless attempt to defy mortality and remain forever young.

The wild spirit of Harry has not been tamed to submission. Revolt may spring up anew, but he now knows that elfland itself has its circumstantial will and that it serves only as a training school for reality.

Harry Richmond and Beauchamp are highly complex romantics. In *The Amazing Marriage* and *Lord Ormont and His Aminta*—and in the romantic scenes in *The Egoist, Diana of the Crossways,* and *One of Our Conquerors*—Meredith was contented with a simple contrast between romance and egoism or sentimentality.

Begun by 1879 and completed in 1895, *The Amazing Marriage* starts off in a spirit of exuberant adventure.[21] Dame Gossip is breathless as she attempts to keep pace with the story of the Old Buccaneer, who at a great age has carried off a dullard's wife, adored her, and lived to mourn her death. The pace slows somewhat as their daughter's tale begins. Carinthia, first seen at dawn leaving her home in the mountains, is a naïve but courageous and resourceful girl of physical vigor and intense enthusiasm. Having no awareness of egosim, she almost immediately accepts the transitorily ardent protestations of the world-weary, sentimental Fleetwood. Treated by him with contempt and then abandoned, she yet remains loyal to the idea of husband and even wields a stick in defending him from the mob. When, after giving him every chance of vindication, she has to reject his best gesture of repentance, she still has not lost her idealism and she can in time marry

Owain Wythan, one of Meredith's dozen or so incarnations of masculine understanding.

In spite of the author's insistence that the excitement-loving Dame Gossip must not have her way, that the action must yield to analysis of minds and hearts, the dame is generally triumphant. Though the last part lacks the buoyant gusto of the earlier writing, it is still a rapid series of incidents. The novelist gave sufficient analysis of Fleetwood's thoughts and motives to make his actions somewhat plausible, but he provided little psychological motivation for Carinthia. She acts in a given way mainly because the theme requires that she do so. As she walks away from her mountain home we feel that we know her because we sense her attachment to the memory of her parents and of her childhood. In England, however, she is hardly more than an allegorical personification, a Britomart, who can err in expecting of others her own excellence, but must eventually triumph because she has no wavering in intent from her romantic ideal.

A much bolder theme is presented in *Lord Ormont and His Aminta,* 1894, as well as a greater daring in its execution. Again, as in *The Amazing Marriage,* sentimentalism is the antagonist; Aminta is the enchanted princess who must escape. In *Farina* Margarita, as we have seen, wove Siegfried's portrait in the tapestry to look singularly like Farina. In *Lord Ormont* Aminta as a school girl likes Matey Weyburn and when old enough to marry weds his soldier hero. The disillusionment is again, as for Carinthia with Fleetwood and Clara Middleton with Sir Willoughby, a test of sympathetic imagination. Aminta endures Ormont's refusal to present her as his wife to society. It is only when she finds that in his pique against society he will reverse his tactics and make her his tool for display of pride that she is free to leave him.

As in the other novels, there are adventurous incidents, including a chase and a rescue from a roué villain. But the most amazing scene is the one in which Weyburn sees Aminta swimming and dives from his boat to join her. A spin of the blood is what Meredith wants to give us. During it the two carry on a poetic conversation, a courtship in which for a few minutes they feel liberated from all the restraints of earth. It is a mature Aminta who, having been deprived by Ormont of her normal adolescent joy, regains girlhood with Weyburn and then as his mistress joins him in starting a boys' school in Switzerland. Once a little ashamed of him as a prospective teacher—it was he who had made her idolize a soldier's career—she now recognizes the romance of his intellectual courage. Again a young woman has come to rediscover freedom and companionship in maturity. For Aminta, as for Keats, life has been a process of "soul making."

Whereas Meredith's study of comic characters of sentimental tinge involved primarily a presentation of their social milieu, the romantic portraits, as one would expect, were accentuated by descriptions of nature. His romantic women are sometimes described in metaphors drawn from nature, and such diverse heroines as Emilia, Carinthia, Diana, Clara, and Aminta are invariably at home in the open air. For both men and women nature supplies the norm. It teaches the freeing of man's spirit from artificial restraints, from sentimental egoism; and at the same time it tests ideals in actuality. For the romantic heroes and heroines the Siegfrieds of tapestries have had to become the Farinas of actual life. The world has not bent to their wishes; dry sedges have remained dry. But the sixty-six-year-old novelist, who had suffered the usual sorrows and frustrations, still believed as firmly as at the age of twenty-three in a beauty that "makes holy earth and air."

Chapter Six

Beauchamp's Quixotic Career

What are we first? First animals; and next
Intelligences at a leap; on whom
Pale lies the distant shadow of the tomb,
And all that draweth on the tomb for text.
(Modern Love)

THE HONOR of England, he felt, had been insulted, and the boy Nevil Beauchamp would take up the gauntlet. Yet how to address a challenge to the officers of the French Guard! For lack of a solution the message was never sent. But the gallant enthusiasm which inspired it was never to be conquered—the "English boyishness, with the novel blush of the heroical nonsensical in it," which made his self-appointed godmother Rosamund, and indeed all women, love him.

Between this first glimpse of the romantic idealist and the final incident, the tossing of his life away to rescue a waif of the mud flats, we have what with comic ambiguity Meredith has called his hero's career. It includes his being whirled from the ground on the blades of windmills and his chasing madly after will-o-the-wisps; but it includes too the bringing of giants to their knees and the exploration of some of the bogs of social England. His career is not, of course, an orderly progress toward the gaining of wisdom. Rather it is a perpetual adventure, with folly coming as well late as early and with prudence learned through mistakes being of little avail against new kinds of temptation to error. When a substantial number of man's chief errors have been explored and the resilience of youthful idealism has been sufficiently tested, Beauchamp's adventures can be brought to a climactic end.

As we have seen, Meredith liked a struggle of ideas. In his greatest romantic novel, *Beauchamp's Career,* 1876, he portrayed idealism in search of a home. As an artist he was concerned with the struggle as it took on physical embodiment in beings who were "first animals; and next intelligences at a leap." As a follower of the Comic Spirit he believed that we must be able to laugh at those whom we love "without loving them less." The story of Beauchamp in fulfilling his requirements has no wholly new elements. We recognize Shibli or Farina, Evan, Harry, or the lad Richard Feverel in his features. There are also at times loose connections between one episode in his life and another, as there were for Evan and Richard and especially for Harry. But what makes *Beauchamp's Career* a more significant story than the previous romantic comedies is the complexity of the hero's aspirations and the intricate interrelations of the different worlds in which he simultaneously tries to live. More ideas than for Evan or indeed for Harry are battling in and around him. Meredith's own casual summary of his novel as he was revising it in June, 1874, is not at all complete and it minimizes Beauchamp's adventure, but it indicates the author's conscious attempt to relate Beauchamp directly to the culture of the novelist's own age:

> It is philosophical-political, with no powerful stream of adventure: an attempt to show the forces round a young man of the present day, in England, who would move them, and finds them unutterably solid, though it is seen in the end that he does not altogether fail, has not lived

> quite in vain.—Of course, this is done in the concrete. A certain drama of self-conquest is gone through, for the hero is not perfect. He is born of the upper class, and is scarcely believed in by any class, except when he vexed his own, and it is then to be hated. At the same time the mild spirit of a prosperous middle class, that is not extremely alarmed, is shown to be above persecuting; so that the unfortunate young man is in danger of being thought dull save by those who can enter his idea of the advancement of Humanity and his passion for it. In this he is a type. And I think his History a picture of the time—taking its mental action, and material ease, and indifference, to be a necessary element of the picture.[22]

The boy who tries to construct the challenge has gone to sea at fourteen years of age and has returned with a dislike for war; he would convert men by argument, not battle. But he is by nature an impulsive fighter. In defense of Rosamund's honor he has trounced his cousin Cecil Baskelett, and before the main action of the novel gets started he has fought in the Crimea while opposing the war itself and despising England's Moslem allies. It is, in fact, characteristic of Beauchamp that he finds himself committed to actions which involve inconsistency. Meredith chose to make the interest of his story reside in the conflict between love and respect for his hero and amusement and vexation at his absurdities. The more inconsistent and comic Beauchamp is, the greater must be his romantic excellence for him to win our respect. In words which would have fitted Evan and the others, the novelist has stressed the naturalness of his hero and by implication the subtle problem of his portrayal:

> Beauchampism . . . may be said to stand for nearly everything which is the obverse of Byronism, and rarely woos your sympathy, shuns the statuesque pathetic, or any kind of posturing. . . . His [Beauchamp's] faith is in working and fighting. With every inducement to offer himself for a

> romantic figure, he despises the pomades and curling-irons of modern romance. . . .

The plan of Meredith's career for Beauchamp makes explicit the novelist's sense of originality:

> Meanwhile the exhibition of a hero whom circumstances overcome, and who does not weep or ask you for a tear, who continually forfeits attractiveness by declining to better his own fortunes, must run the chances of a novelty. . . .

Thackeray and Dickens portrayed un-Byronic heroes who yielded to circumstance, so that the novelty is not unique. The subject of Meredith's story is nevertheless original.

A Meredithian novel will very seldom follow a straight course in pursuit of the hero. To understand Beauchamp's restiveness and dilemmas we must learn of the culture in which he has been reared; and so the author can seem to forget Beauchamp for a while to give us a portrait of the lad's uncle and guardian, Everard Romfrey, third son of an earl. It was characteristic of Englishmen, Meredith felt, to take personal pride in being related to heroes. Willoughby was to glamorize his distant cousin in the marines; Everard Romfrey is proud of his soldier nephew. He approves the war on grounds of patriotism; Meredith himself says that England supported the Turks partly because they were good customers. Romfrey protests against a cotton spinner, presumably Bright, who has opposed war, and he has other reasons for dislike of the cotton manufacturers: they overwork children, sing Sunday tunes, agitate concerning the corn laws, and protect poachers. In short, their interests are contradictory to the well-established aristocratic traditions by which Romfrey survives and they are therefore unpatriotic. While yet in England Beauchamp has pitted his immature talent for debate against his uncle's convictions and in so doing has announced the principles of the crusade to which he will return. But the youth himself is of the leisured upper classes and Romfrey has not held against him his adolescent rebellion against Tory-Whig ideals. He likes his nephew and is glad to find that, however odd his political whims, he is a gallant British soldier. Were it not that the hunting season is opening, he would himself go to Italy with his housekeeper Rosamund to visit the lad, who is there for convalescence from fever.

Beauchamp needs several foils for the proper portrayal of his character, and the one who serves best is Romfrey, who is a "crotchety unintelligible Whig" regarded by Radicals as a Tory. At one time the author calls him "a medieval gentleman with the docile notions of the twelfth century, complacently driving them to grass and wattling them in the nineteenth." In the abstract the Romfreys of England, whether Whig or Tory, are reaction epitomized. Overworking of children may distress them, but parasitism of the aristocracy and upper-middle class upon the poor does not. As an individual, Everard Romfrey is a mixture of the ridiculous and the heroic. In defense of his position he can try to outwit Beauchamp and, when Rosamund has misrepresented Dr. Shrapnel's words to her, he can horsewhip the man. Yet when proved wrong he can make an honorable and humble apology; also he has a fair sense of humor, and, above all, he loves Beauchamp. Had he followed his principles he would soon have cast the youth off as a traitor and a fool. Instead he endures his radicalism and even when most wrathful against him feels an anxious longing for reconcilement. As Meredith was anti-Tory, his characterization of Romfrey, like that of Beauchamp, gave him an opportunity to test his skill. It would have been a simple matter of Dickensian perspective to make Romfrey a caricature, an almost equally simple one to sentimentalize him. Meredith instead gives him the same comic scathing that he gives his hero, that he may be somewhat purified by the ordeal.

It is with a history of mental revolt against Romfreyism and with disillusionment about the war that Beauchamp comes to his first test. With Meredith, whatever be the age and the spirit of his heroes, there is always, as if suspended above their heads, where they do not see it but we do, the motto that "the love-season is the carnival of egoism, and it brings the touchstone to our natures." The fact that a man or woman was not limited exclusively to love one person did not trouble the novelist. That there should be some false starts before men and women were ready for enduring affection and that love of one did not exclude admiration of others accorded with his belief that soul develops in man and that civilization is ideally a reaching out toward others instead of an inhibiting confinement of interest to one object or person possessed. If the finding of a sympathetic mind was in itself a complex quest demanding an education of its own, the problem was infinitely expanded by the fact that love could not be separated from all other things in one's life. It was for Meredith the test of the validity of one's convictions and of the seriousness with which one held them, yet it was not all-dominating in the life of the average man. Though in a tragedy the hero may heroically give up all for love and go magnificently to death, we must remember that even Antony has other interests besides Cleopatra. In a comedy love may be the main or only interest. But for most men, as Browning implied, there is never meeting at night without parting to do the world's work in the morning. Meredith would agree with Browning.

In the first love scene in *Beauchamp's Career* the novelist presents man in his typical egoistic inconsistency. It is characteristic of male egoism, according to Meredith's concept of that inevitable disease, that from his beloved the lover should demand a meeting at night as if the world did not otherwise exist for her and she were to accept his way of life forever. But as for himself, except for a moment, man has no intention of giving up his work in the world. Indeed he has made sure of completing his eight hours before turning to thought of his beloved, and he can love her beyond all else provided that she believes in his work and will yield to its demands. By work we must, of course, here understand Beauchamp's endeavors to revolt against the social state of mankind and to remold society in the pattern of his own revolt.

The Beauchamp who has already gone on walks with a country lass in England, is later to be argumentatively in love with Cecilia Halkett, and will finally marry Jenny Denham, asks of the seventeen-year-old Renée de Croisnel what Meredith believed that even the most idealistic and gallant of men expect of women. The French culture which has fostered Renée presents Beauchamp with a paradox which is to typify his career. The young Englishman is almost enchanted not only by Renée but by what is to him a strange new culture; his imagination and sensations can luxuriate. But at the same time his intellect, supported by the instinct of a lover, begins to rebel against the Tory-like conservatism of this culture and especially against what he interprets as its enslavement of women. And so, merely through the seemingly casual juxtaposition of conflicting impressions, Meredith has set before us a type of mental conflict which epitomizes Beauchamp's career.

In his preface to *The Princess Casamassima* Henry James enunciates the principle on which an interesting character is to be built. The character must for James be sensitive and intelligent and yet not to the point where he can be too knowing. The problem for the artist, according to James here and elsewhere, is to keep the protagonist in the right degree of perplexity and, while letting him develop awareness, to make the reader share enlightenment on his problems too. In Beauchamp we have a good example of what James meant. What from our vantage at the end of the novel we can analyze omnisciently we have actually learned only as we have watched a sensitive hero illustrate it. We have been as perplexed as he was, and only through his growth have we ourselves achieved an awareness which in some respects goes beyond his own.

For Beauchamp to accept the traditions of the new civilization which delights him means to approve of Renée's marrying a middle-aged man whom she scarcely respects. With his hero's condemnation of the system the author, as we at once see, is in accord; from her marriage Renée can anticipate bitter sorrow. But Beauchamp with the unbending determination of a reforming rebel would tear her away from her family culture, oblivious of the fact that her strangeness and charm are inseparable from it. She must in effect renounce her heritage and accept his. But what can he offer when he asks her to go with him instead of returning to her father and her fiancé? He has attempted to revolt against his own family traditions, so that he cannot consistently bring her to England and introduce her into a society at all comparable to that which she must give up. Though he never stops to reason about the matter while pleading with her, we come in time to see that he could not really carry her off to some idyllic retreat from the world's injustices, for he is the same Beauchamp who will later refuse to do precisely that when she desperately asks him to. Instead of heroically and impractically leading her away—and Meredith inserts the plausible comment that she would passively have acquiesced—he joins the ranks of the novelist's comic lovers by demanding that she decide for herself, that she prove her courage and maturity of judgment by renouncing family and position to gamble all on faith in a young man without prospects and with an unsettled, impetuous mind. She is, in short, to demonstrate her independence by renouncing it; for, once she has voluntarily chosen to go with Beauchamp, she will be irrevocably dependent upon his unproved talents and his uncertain will. That Beauchamp should make such a request of Renée shows how deep in tradition and perhaps in human nature itself Meredith believed the subjugation of women to have its roots.

For Beauchamp what happens is probably best, though Rosamund later repents her part in it. With gentle persistence she exerts just enough persuasion to prevent heroic folly. Her motives are mixed, to be sure, as they continue to be throughout the story. Beauchamp is the only person she fully loves, and she will immolate herself determinedly for his happiness, but she fears any act which by alienating him from Romfrey would put him beyond her sacrificial control. She is here sentimentally comic, imaginative only to the point of apprehending the danger of change, and yet fundamentally sound in that she senses the very things which do control men's lives, even when they most deny them. The two lovers are opposed in interests and immature. Though her discovery that Beauchamp loves her changes her from a dreaming girl to a woman, Renée still pleads her inexperience, which, we are to discover, she will finally outgrow through suffering. And with all his nobility and generosity, Beauchamp is yet no mature lover of the court of love tradition, but an impulsive carnivalist who will at another time be an equally impulsive ascetic. The comedy of his actions is the more subtle in that all turns out as Meredith believes that it should, and yet it is the unheroic rather than the sublime which has triumphed.

There is no comedy, of course, in the anguish of Renée. Her father represents the assumption of his class that individuality must be confined to the decorous cultivation in a dilettante way of one's interest in the arts. Emotion for him must yield to one's concept of gentlemanly manners, a concept at once able to encompass immorality and rigorous propriety. The fiancé is an "ogre straining at an Adonis." Renée is helpless; when Beauchamp does not force her to elope she cannot herself break away, and she must submit to the tyrannic pattern which society has set.

The world which Beauchamp has been allowed to glimpse is fascinating, yet sinister. To challenge the officers of the French Guard was nothing when compared to battling the spirit of the race, which everywhere confronts him with politely ruthless indifference. But on his return to fight for his causes in England Beauchamp cannot forget France. A distinguishing feature of his career is that he never casts aside one burden when he adds a new one, no matter how irreconcilable they may be.

Although the incidents to this point are of great importance, their function is much like that of a prologue. Were the novel a picaresque tale these events would merely be behind Beauchamp when he suddenly returns to England to start afresh. In external structure Meredith's novel has, particularly at this juncture, the same loose relationship as a picaresque story, even as his other novels so often have. But what the novelist has given is the boyhood and youthful characteristics which will now find ampler and more intricate expression even when Beauchamp attempts to put his youth behind him.

The history of his renewed life in England can be interpreted from divers views. In one sense it is an ironic study of man's rebellion against circumstance and of his illusion of being the master of his fate. When Beauchamp would like to believe that he is free to shape his career, some one else, usually a woman—Rosamund, Renée, Cecilia Halkett, or Jenny Denham—will unexpectedly do something which counteracts his plans. He is always to draw near to victory only to be snatched away by his hovering goddess and set down to fight a fresh enemy in a new part of the field.

From a second perspective the story is a study of the conflict of allegiances, comparable to the medieval type involving one's lord, one's lady, and one's spiritual quest, except that for the author of *The Shaving of Shagpat* the dilemmas are inevitably intricate and comic.

Romfrey is Beauchamp's rightful lord. To him he owes a gratitude which weighs heavily on his mind. He has accepted Romfrey's largesse, enjoyed the luxury and the prestige which his uncle has given him, and become so much at home in the upper-middle class and aristocratic environment that he cannot desert it even in revolt. But Romfrey has a casual cynicism in politics and is tenaciously attached to the *status quo*. He assumes that class interests will always remain irreconcilable and hopes merely to stock Parliament with enough members of his own persuasion. To give him the devotion Beauchamp would like to give and yet preserve his own principles, the youth must conquer his lord, by argument, to be sure, that he may voluntarily surrender after victory. The conflict between head and heart is of heroic implications, but the author resists the temptation to renounce his comic perspective. In deploring Byronic characterizations and "modern romance" he did not mean that his story was unromantic. What he opposed was histrionic exhibitionism and unpsychological glamorizing of heroes. By avoiding one single tremendous scene in which Beauchamp would defy Romfrey while loyal to him he may have rejected a type of incident common to actuality. But he found that he could better illuminate the complexity of Beauchamp's conflict by avoiding a dramatic explosion.

To prevent his nephew's winning a seat in Parliament and there announcing opinions which would be annoying, Romfrey supports the worthless Cecil Baskelett for the office. To run Cecil was "conscienceless of course. But that was the way of the Old School." Though he once fought to defend a woman's honor, Romfrey can unchivalrously try to get Cecilia wedded to Cecil, whom he really despises. Again, when Cecilia is affianced to Blackburn Tuckham, Romfrey would have her renounce him for Beauchamp or at least for a while pretend to do so. Such surrender to expediency is, to be sure, astonishing, and it would be impossible for Beauchamp to compromise with it. But he must have someone to believe in. As a boy he chose as his favorite author "one [Carlyle] writing of Heroes," and he needs a hero to champion. He finds in the radical seer Dr. Shrapnel the hero which he could not make of Romfrey. Shrapnel, a tall, "carelessly clad" man, is the antithesis of "that amiable nobility whose pretensions were comically built on birth, acres, tailoring, style, and an air." At times Shrapnel is much like Meredith himself, both in his ideals and in his habits. A democrat, he finds a musical analogy, using one of the novelist's own favorite metaphors; the organ is inferior to the orchestra, which requires an affinity of minds. He is a vegetarian, as Meredith was too for a while. Unlike the author he damns capital, but Meredith did deplore the abuses of parasitism. The letter which Shrapnel writes to Beauchamp is a strongly-worded demand for improvement of economic, political, and religious conditions in England. Cecil mocks its style, but the conservative Seymour Austin separates the actually mild and reasonable recommendations from the wild rhetoric in which they are shrouded.

Shrapnel is really a kindly, gentlemanly, and patient man; but Beauchamp is drawn to him as if he were the ascetic embodiment of Beauchamp's ideals. He accepts the doctor's views, including the vegetarianism, and works himself into a crusading excitement for them. Above all, he would fain be loyal to both Romfrey and Shrapnel instead of finding his two allegiances at war. This aspect of his life culminates with his career itself. When Rosamund has timidly misrepresented Shrapnel and caused Romfrey to whip him, Beauchamp insists on an apology. It is to keep her from going herself that Romfrey, now an earl, goes instead and in so doing wins his nephew's unqualified affection. Soon after, in thinking back over what Meredith now labels "Beauchamp's career," the earl adds good-naturedly, "But one thing he did do: *he got me down on my knees!*" As with the Capulets and Montagues, Romfrey and Shrapnel are united as they walk away from the beach at the very end.

Beauchamp's relations with women are perhaps the most un-Byronic elements of his career. Handsome and gallant of manner, he is popular among women, and at least four are in love with him at one time. But his treatment of them is not only not seductive; it is obtusely the opposite, for his Italian romance with Renée sets the tone for all his courtship of her and of Cecilia and Jenny. His attitude is superficially the antithesis of the popular Victorian adaptation of courtly love. He puts no woman on the heights, transforms none into a star to guide his wandering bark, is not a votive pilgrim at love's shrine. Instead he argues for a woman's support of his ideas as if he were canvassing for a vote at the polls, and he even takes love for granted. Virtue in distress finds in him a determined champion; but instead of breakng the door to rescue the imprisoned damsel, he may instruct her, passionately to be sure, on how to file the bars of her window and let herself down outside. What he does finally learn about wooing comes after Jenny has decided to marry him and mainly after the marriage itself.

That the author thinks Beauchamp far superior to the kind of lover who makes love all sentiment is, of course, implicit. The youth at his best is not lowering but elevating the position of women. At the same time, there is a male egoism about him which Meredith finds amusing, and there is comedy too in the way the women feel drawn toward him by his demands that they be independent, yet shrink from or even fight against independence. They want to be treated as persons loved; moreover they want to admire a lover, not to be decried by their associates while trying to defend his political views, in which they have no personal interest.

Despite their differences, all the women have in common certain characteristics which Meredith believed inherent in their semi-cloistered positions. Rosamund, not yet middleaged, is a widow living under the protection of Romfrey. She has a good sense of humor, and the author makes a point of the fact that she is not unduly sentimental. Yet she gets herself into awkward situations because of her timid, indirect machinations. Loving Beauchamp, she schemes to marry him to the conventional Cecilia and establish him as the respectable heir of his uncle. She is far more attracted by the French grace of Renée, but especially after Renée's marriage she fears an attachment that might further unsettle the already turbulent life and reputation of Beauchamp. She devotedly nurses Renée through the illness which succeeds Beauchamp's rejection of her, but she also admits relief at that rejection. The supreme irony and confusion for her is that she, gently as always, creates circumstances that suggest to Romfrey the chivalry of marrying her, her intention being thereby to help Beauchamp become reinstated as heir, and then discovers that her devotion will be rendered vain by the birth of a direct heir.

Though as a lad Beauchamp championed Rosamund with his fists and though he turns to her for help, he refuses to understand her. He cannot, for example, comprehend her fears concerning Renée, and he blames her for her conventional standards. Yet when Renée comes to London, the young radical asks Rosamund to come at once to make Renée's visit seem proper. He is indeed at heart much more conventional than Rosamund. Nor can he see that she would naturally be frightened by the stories about Shrapnel's radicalism and that she would therefore be prejudiced against Jenny, his ward. He knows only that she has misrepresented the man by not denying Cecil's assertion that Shrapnel insulted her, and he demands that she restore her honor by speaking the truth. Her courage in admitting her falsehood is much greater than he perceives, as he judges her—and all others—as if she were himself. Perhaps Rosamund would have been apprehensive if Beauchamp had ever given signs of really appreciating her feelings, for she was, after all, much older than he; there are some things that are very serious in a woman's life and yet might be misconstrued by a young man as comic.

It is on the eve of election, when Beauchamp should be bringing his campaign to a climax, that there arrives the one-word telegram from Renée—"Come." For Beauchamp there is no choice, and he hurries to France. In the scenes that follow Meredith has stressed how little even a generous person such as his hero can enter imaginatively into the life of another. The cause of the telegram was a mere wager of a glove by Renée; if he did not arrive within the hour named the glove would be forfeit to her admirer D'Henriel. There is no frank conversation between Renée and Beauchamp. Only by fragmentary bits does he learn, mainly from Mme. d'Auffray, her sister-in-law, the invidious cause of the wager. The husband, intent on his own pleasures, has left his sister to guard Renée, and Mme. d'Auffray, knowing the emptiness of her life, has permitted amusement; but when the conduct of D'Henriel threatens peril, she encourages the venture of the glove, for her brother is jealous of no one but Beauchamp and only his presence will bring the roué home.

The damning picture of *mariage de convenance* is interesting for its own sake. The perplexity of Beauchamp is a severe test for his idealism. He even longs for disillusionment about Renée; she has torn him from his career without the least concern for it. When he tries to be serious at her table by attacking duelling, he is considered by the company to be discourteous. There is no outlet for his ideas, and his hostess has prevented any hint of love. If Beauchamp had read Ovid he would have agreed that love disintegrates a man's character. He is a knight-errant trapped in the bower of bliss: "he by blood a racer; and his nature craved for diversions, against his will, against his moral sense and born tenacity of spirit." He feels in a land of "whirlwinds catching the wits, and whipping the passions." As he learns of Mme. d'Auffray's duplicity he is increasingly bewildered and shocked:

> He stood divided between a sense of the bubbling shallowness of the life about him, and a thought, grave as an eye dwelling on blood, of sinister things below it . . . he felt oddly entangled.

The bower of bliss is, in fact, a wretched place, not in the least idyllic. The lovers go on an excursion, during which the intrusive D'Henriel contributes low comedy by falling head first into the water and Renée is astonished when an over-swollen gourd reminds her of her husband. But she is ashamed of having found amusement with D'Henriel and wants her lover to accuse her harshly that he may then sympathize. Though Meredith does not say so, it is clear that her guilt is from disloyalty to Beauchamp, a fact which he himself never comprehends. Instead he condemns the social system in which she lives and expects her to free herself somehow from it.

The scene is given either as pure drama or as it is interpreted by Beauchamp, and the reader's shock of awareness is the greater because he sees Renée only through her actions. She treats her guest as if she were a coquette staking a glove on her power over him, and she follows each kindness with aloofness. But in this instance the reader, at first as ignorant as Beauchamp, suddenly outstrips him by perceiving that the girl is frightened because she is in love.

The Renée who later arrives in London is helpless and humiliated. The roué husband has chosen to become her lover, and it is to avoid utter self-scorn that she flees to Beauchamp to beg him to take her away. We see little of Renée in this scene. Rosamund comes when telegraphed, and soon Mme. d'Auffray appears, followed by her brother. Meredith deliberately removed his heroine from the stage, it would seem, that we should not have anticlimactic dialogue between her and Beauchamp after the latter has treated her not in the manner of a lover, but as an embarrassed father confessor. It is true that he has written her to depend on him for help, but at the time of his vague offer he was already repenting his earlier folly and, besides, his allowance from Romfrey had stopped. In Italy he asked Renée to give up the world for him; she is now ready. With no interest in his work, she now sees love as an eternal devotion of each to the other. She has thrown herself at his feet, not doubting that he will pick her up; she has come, she says, to prove her courage. But when, sensing her mistake, she asks whether she is a burden, Beauchamp cannot truthfully say no. Naïvely he remarks, "You are alone: and you have told me nothing." He equivocates that he loves her, but he is thinking of his moral obligation to the world, and he even hears Dr. Shrapnel disapproving. He lectures her that young women need society. When she protests, he shakes his head "paternally." Her response keeps us reminded of the fact that laughter intensifies pathos: "Her instinct of comedy set a dimple working in her cheek. 'Not if they love, Nevil'."

Renée has pictured her lover as "one flash of blood-warm welcome awaiting her." Yet the most gallant phrase he can muster is that he will see her "through it," and his practical concern for what his political enemies may make of his conduct brings forth, "And if they can get me . . ." Mark Antony would not have hesitated; by contrast with what he believes that chivalry demands Beauchamp feels himself ludicrous. Actually he never has renounced the world and its conventions, nor does Meredith disapprove because he has not. Though we learn afterward that upon recovery from the nearly fatal shock the girl resigns herself to finding comfort in religion while she lives a dead life, Meredith will accept no gentler verdict, for Beauchamp must do his work in the world. Had he abandoned his work he could never have concealed from Renée that she was the burden that had destroyed his career. Instead he keeps her respect and during his illness she returns to England to visit him.

In Renée, Meredith depicted one of his most profound and tragic heroines, worthy of a complete novel to herself, and he remarked years later that he was still a little in love with her. The comic irony—and the pathos—is in the fact that she should submit to being lessoned in moral philosophy by a mere page in the Court of Love.

Cecilia has none of the fascination of Renée. The daughter of a reactionary, she has been reared to what Beauchamp, identifying her with her expensive yacht, calls a "beautiful servicelessness." She has lived in wealthy detachment from social problems and when she becomes fond of Beauchamp she wants to lift him off the earth onto her cloud. His canvassing is not heroic to her; she thinks of it as "slime." In tolerant moments Beauchamp pictures her as suited for a happy home life; but long before he considers marrying her he has tried to make her subscribe to his ideas. Later, instead of speaking of love he insists that she listen to Dr. Shrapnel's voluminous letter, and Cecilia objects to such oblique wooing. The scene contrasts favorably with sentimental courtships, but Beauchamp is none the less an insensitive egoist:

> He wanted in fact a ready-made heroine, and did not give her credit for the absence of fire in her blood, as well as for the unexercised imagination which excludes young women from the power to realize unwonted circumstances. We men walking about the world have perhaps no more imagination of matters not domestic than they; but what we have is quick with experience: we see the thing we hear of: women come to it how they can.

A conventional girl, Cecilia is enthralled by a portrait of Renée and yet annoyed by her unconventional pose. She does begin to argue on politics, giving Beauchamp credit for her ideas, but she cannot any more than Renée break away from her heritage without help. It is assumed by her father and friends that she must marry; and when Beauchamp does not ask her, she accepts the conservative Tuckham, though disturbed by his overbearing manner and ungraceful figure. It is indeed a blow to her when the middle-aged, sympathetic Seymour Austin, to whom her heart has turned, pleads for

Tuckham instead of himself. Minutes late in proposing, Beauchamp blames circumstance:

> You have known I love you. I have been distracted by things . . . and love's a selfish business while . . . [*sic.*] while one has work in hand. It's clear I can't do two things at a time—make love and carry on my taskwork. . . . I believed you were mine and wanted no lovemaking. There's no folly in that if you understand me at all.

Though pledged to Tuckham, Cecilia quits eating meat when Beauchamp does, and there is no doubt of the secret she will keep in her heart. More important, through losing Beauchamp she finally comes to see that she has been selfish in her imagined idealism, that "the aim at an ideal life closely approaches, or easily inclines, to self-worship." She has been guilty of "adoring her own image," but now she is freed of that sin: "What was this ideal she had complained of losing? It was a broken mirror: she could think of it in no other form." As Beauchamp has never in his thoughts managed to separate Cecilia from her environment, she has learned far more from him than he has from her. She might have drifted into something akin to the sentimental cloistral-harem existence Meredith was later to depict for Constance Asper, had the young radical not jarred her into reality.

Despite the schooling he has had, Beauchamp comes to Jenny Denham still far from learned. Jenny is the one who completes his education. Simple in manner and attire, she has yet a French quality in her dress suggestive of Renée, and as the disciple of the sensible Lydiard she has views on politics. But she also knows the dangers of megalomania. When Beauchamp speaks of his "battle without end," she replies shrewdly, "But does incessant battling keep the intellect clear?"

Jenny's subjugation of Beauchamp is pure comedy. He proposes marriage by explaining that Dr. Shrapnel would not want her left alone in the world. Jenny, however, insists on a term of courtship. When she queries whether "we ourselves are using reason rightly, Nevil—not prejudice," he stops her argument with a kiss and assures her paternally that he will always listen to her, "whether she Lydiardized, or what Dr. Shrapnel called Jennyprated." The eternal egoism, Meredith seems to say, defies restraint. But Jenny counters with words that speak for many other of the novelist's heroines: "That is to say, dear Nevil, that you have quite made up your mind to a toddling chattering little nursery wife?" Though Beauchamp has denounced the clergy for not helping the poor, the two are married not by a consul, as he prefers, but by a minister, and their child is later baptized. "Apparently," Meredith remarks, "the commission of the act of marriage was to force Beauchamp from all his positions one by one." But in summary he adds that Jenny "led him back to those forsaken valleys of his youth. . . . Beauchamp drank of a happiness that neither Renée nor Cecilia had promised." This resumé of their short life together is rather an assertion than proof. It represents, however, the author's own commentary on the need heretofore in his hero's life, a need which only uninhibited intellectual companionship of the sexes could fulfil.

It has been objected against Meredith that he did not really believe in the emancipation of women since he regularly provided them with husbands. The career of Beauchamp even more than the stories of Clara Middleton and Aminta refutes this misconception; it is the young man himself who lacks what only women can give. If most of the action in his history directly or indirectly involves them, it is because the novelist believed that without them the career of his youthful social reformer would have been arid.

We come at last to Beauchamp's work because understanding it depends upon knowing the persons who assist or hamper it and who are benefited by it. What is it that he wants to do? The answer, he believes, is very simple. A boy who would challenge the officers of the French Guard sees life as a knightly adventure of destroying prejudice and social injustice. Reason is clearly distinct from unreason, being its opposite; and once it has outlined a course, all mankind should eagerly follow. Beauchamp's ideal has all the beauty for him that certain of the Round-Table knights dreamed of when they imagined the Holy Grail. Like those knights, he hopes that he will come into the presence of the ideal itself.

In the mid-twentieth century, when the "affective fallacy" is a controversial issue, distinctions have sometimes been drawn between what a work of literature is as an influence upon the reader and what it is as a work of art. Actually the wisdom which the perceptive reader gains from *Beauchamp's Career,* whether it include deeper knowledge of social England or profounder understanding of psychology, is inseparable from appreciation of the art with which the novelist has chosen, arranged, and interpreted his sociological and psychological materials. In tracing the career of the hero we are therefore not oblivious to the art of the telling, for the incidents themselves are the product of selection and imagination, in short, the expression of the novelist's art.

The career of social reformer that Beauchamp has embraced involves, in one perspective, a conflict between the natural indolence of man, which makes him first of all an animal, and the inspiration which comes to him as if in flashes of intellect. In a somewhat higher form it is a conflict of heart and head. In respect to temperament it is often a civil war of Cavaliers and Roundheads within Beauchamp's imagination. What alone permits affirmative resolution of the strife and lets Beauchamp remain active in the world instead of turning to some form of escape is that, with all his folly, he never once tastes of the gall of the Roc. His errors are indeed inseparable from his problems, and Meredith makes quite clear the fact that he really has much less folly than most men. For Beauchamp's and our good, however, he has chosen to lay bare the young man's soul.

Beauchamp would improve the living conditions of the lower classes; he sails on an anti-slavery mission; he would liberate women from the trammels of sentimental conventionality, and he would enfranchise them, at least socially. He attacks the oppressive weight on England of a landed gentry and aristocracy and the sloth of the clergy, which is comfortably secure under the *status quo*. He would free all men from needless restrictions—such as Sunday ordinances—which curtail normal human pleasure and development. He would make politics a frank contest of issues in which reason could examine facts and dispassionately choose the best. None of these views, which are all derived from or endorsed by Shrapnel, are different from Meredith's own. In fact, the novelist gave to Beauchamp and Shrapnel his own beliefs about the social morass of his time.

But in testing these beliefs Meredith has stressed the great difference between simple acceptance of them and the putting them to work. If his hero flounders in confusion and inconsistency he does so because he is no hypocrite. By temperament and rearing he enjoys luxury almost as much as did Harry Richmond. A yacht he considers a virtual necessity for the convalescence of Dr. Shrapnel, and his schemes, including the dream of founding a newspaper, require lavish expenditure. Yet he would like to be ascetically devoted to his cause, and in the midst of eating food specially brought from the country he may suddenly become ashamed of the extravagance. He has no positive plan for raising the standard of living of the poor, and also he assumes naïvely that every poor man is exempt from animal indolence and is a politically advanced thinker. Yet he is completely democratic in spirit and is depressed because he cannot destroy what he knows is unwholesome oppression. Until late he is unable to perceive the excellence of individual women's minds, yet he finds in them his noblest inspiration. In deploring the narrowness of the clergy he has a stereotyped picture of indolent smugness which may be unjust to the clergy, but instead of cynically rejecting their ideas because he rejects the men, he tries to put their preachings into practice.

Beauchamp's main difficulties are two and they are inseparable. He does not understand people, including himself, and, as the wise Rosamund tells Romfrey, "he runs too much from first principles to extremes." He expects everyone to join him as soon as he himself has seen the path. Cecilia must love Shrapnel because he does. When Romfrey has apologized, Jenny must at once see his nobility and forget his rudeness. In politics Beauchamp does not see that Toryism is a habit of living rather than a matter of subscription to party tenets. He never looks at politics in terms of personalities. About to argue with one Oggler to win his vote, he is shocked to learn that, although Oggler already intends to vote for him, his reasons are contemptible. During the campaign his own publicist distressingly insists that facts must give way to expediency, since one cannot do good without first being elected. His running mate, he finally recognizes, is more conservative than his opponents and far less flexible in mind. In fact, the Tories—and Whigs, who are grouped with them in Beauchamp's mind—include not only Romfrey and Cecilia's reactionary father, but Seymour Austin and Stukely Culbrett, both of whom respect Shrapnel and are impressed with his ideas. It is, moreover, Beauchamp's conservative kinsman Tuckham who out of loyalty restores the inheritance which, because of his political integrity, Beauchamp has forfeited.

If, however, Beauchamp is a novice in arms, he is a better, more useful man for his lack of political shrewdness. He cannot win an election, but he does accomplish some things. He succeeds in exposing the motives of those who resist change, and they are less comfortable in their defensive fortresses than before. He has helped to create an atmosphère favorable to emancipation of the socially oppressed and has reminded the church of its function. His influence has been not so much in the inculcation of ideas as in the winning of respect for his sincerity. Politically he has one triumph which Meredith feels is in itself significant. Confronted by Oggler and by men whose votes are for sale, he also meets Carpendike, an independent voter, who argues against his views but votes for him nevertheless. For Meredith the converting of one man by argument and character was in the direction of progress. The influence of Beauchamp on his friends we have already noted. Each is in one way or another inspired by him to act with courage and honor.

Important ultimately is what Beauchamp has done with his own life, for even in its teaching the novel is concerned first with how to live. Meredith was not so unknowing as to suppose that specific legal or social reforms have value apart from human nature. He was really concerned with primary human values. When we think back over Beauchamp's career we perceive that in his steadfast integrity, courage, and enthusiasm he has come about as near as is allowable for man to the ideals which he has sought. He has done so not by retreating from the world as did the seekers of the Grail, but by living in the world exactly as was recommended, we may recall, by Meredith's and Beauchamp's favorite Victorian author, who wrote of heroes with a "wind-in-the-orchard style."

There is poignant romance in Beauchamp's career. Man's quest is his life and as he learns to live he consumes the time yet left for living. His life is composed of fragments, of things never quite completed. Even though an orderly purpose inspires it, his life does not seem to him calm and orderly. It is the function of art, however, to transcend nature. From reading Beauchamp's biography we discover what he himself could never have made articulate. Even his death, which comes from the rescue of an inconspicuous child and the attempt to rescue a second, is part of the artistic pattern. Like the two youths who die in Juliet's tomb or Keats' young lovers who flee away "into the storm," the Beauchamp that we know and want to know has completed his career. We are not interested in an elderly citizen who might have let oddities develop into crotchets and might even have quarreled, as reformers sometimes do, with those who would go yet further. This would not be Meredith's Beauchamp at all. "Smart lad," said Housman of his athlete some twenty years later; Meredith had already said the same. By taking his hero through his ordeal—an ordeal inescapable for a high-minded yet very human lad—he stripped romance of the mawkish sentimentality so pleasing not only to Victorians but to all generations. The beauty which remained is the more poignant because of the shadow upon it of the distant but inevitable tomb.

Chapter Seven

The Rod of the Darker Muse

But nature says: 'My children most they seem
When they least know me: therefore I decree
That they shall suffer!'

(Modern Love)

THE COMIC spirit was so insistent in Meredith that he rarely looked at an important tragic protagonist without seeing his comic incongruity. That he did understand pathos and tragedy in their classic simplicity is evident in brief sketches of minor characters and in the separate episode in his first prose fiction, in which he told the story of Bhanavar the Beautiful. Thereafter, even in the short tale of Chloe, he mixed his tones, and so, after *The Shaving of Shagpat,* we must not expect simplicity of design.

As life usually consists of a mixture of tragedy, romance, and comedy, Meredith would test his artistic skill by encompassing all three in the same canvas. It is this determination which accounts for his major originality—the exploration of the tragicomic—but also for the diffuseness which disturbs those who think of Aeschylus and Sophocles as the standards of unity. Certainly it is responsible for that amalgam *Diana of the Crossways,* which could have been a tragedy and instead ended with Indian-summer romance. It weakens the story of Chloe, and while expanding the epic proportions of *Rhoda Fleming,* prevents the author from pursuing the tragedy to its most intense resolution. Actually in the "Tale of Bhanavar the Beautiful" Meredith showed that in simple tragedy he could find ample range, and it is unfortunate that he never chose to restrict himself so completely again.

Like the comic parts of *The Shaving of Shagpat,* to which it is related only in that the knowledge of tragedy is necessary for Shibli's complete education, the tale of Bhanavar is in the form of an oriental allegory. The adventures are fantastic; the serpents and the transformations are supernatural. The reality of the story lies consequently in its implications, for the author chose human passions for his subject, together with the relentless consequences of their expression.

Bhanavar is of the tradition of fatal ladies who are yet pathetic in their sinister destinies. At her request the youth Zurven ravishes a jewel from the forehead of the Serpent of the Lake. Bitten by the dying serpent, he dies too; but before death he warns that the jewel is "the giver of years and of powers, and of loveliness beyond mortal, yet the wearing of it availeth not in the pursuit of happiness." Soon Bhanavar is to lament:

> Destiny! Destiny! why am I so dark [evil]?
> I that have beauty and love to be fair.

In her magic loveliness she is a deadly attraction for men. As Ruark, her new lover, says:

> Long we the less, the less, woe's me!
> Because thou art deathly,—the less for thee?

Taken from Ruark, she is for a while happy with Almeryl. When he is put to death she renounces love and thinks of her beauty only as the means of luring her enemy, the Vizier, to give her the kiss which will insure his death.

With revenge achieved she has only power to long for. As the queen of Mashalleed she will use her beauty—always dependent on the jewel—to make the king a "stepping-stone to power, rejoicing my soul with the shock of armies." In the war which she inspires she has Ruark captured. Desire for power and memory of love are confusedly mingled in her mind. Never, even in the days with Almeryl, was she able to love without fear and reservation, and now she is inextricably in the toils of the serpents. Her beauty gives way to the features of a hag, and the serpents demand that with a kiss she prepare a soul as sacrifice for Karatis. She would kiss the king, whom she despises, but helplessly kisses Ruark instead. Her beauty is instantly renewed, but in horror at what she has done she tries to slay the serpents who have come for Ruark and, that being vain, she casts the jewel from her. Her last thought is to rescue Ruark and restore him to his mother, the woman whose suspicion was in part the cause of her sorrow. An hour later the king's guards lay before him the lovers' heads:

> Mashalleed gazed upon the head of Bhanavar and sighed, for death had made the head again fair with a wondrous beauty, a loveliness never before seen on earth.

The tragic katharsis of egoism is implicit. It is not love but the possession of love which Bhanavar has earlier known, not the love of beauty but vanity in its possession, not adventure but power to control men's actions. All these, which have brought her shame and remorse, vanish in her one self-forgetful act, the attempt at rescue. It is not difficult to translate her story into the terms of modern life or to apply the aphoristic verses which provide its choral comment.

Meredith did not lose interest in Bhanavar when he brought his fiction to English settings and substituted nineteenth-century prose for the quaint lines of Anglicized oriental romance. In various avatars the fatal lady reappears and demands our pity. Bella Mountfalcon is very much a beautiful witch, who with serpent cunning fascinates Richard Feverel. Like Bhanavar she feels herself a creature of evil destiny, and like her she renounces evil when she is transformed by love; but the evil consequences she too cannot prevent.

Margaret Lovell in *Rhoda Fleming* has let her husband fight and be killed because of the power of her beauty over men. After describing her blond loveliness Meredith adds, "There is a fate attached to some women . . . that blood is to be shed for them." In her frustrate desire for action Mrs. Lovell has since gambled away most of her property; she would even welcome a chance to gamble men's lives, and she would be astonished, the author tells us, were the victims to demur. In a world where she feels that only men can act with forthright power she resorts to dependence on her beauty and wiles. She refuses to marry the one man who has loved her enough to rebuke her folly and instead accepts the hand of a banker of wealth and approaching senility. To the unsophisticated Fleming girls she is a strange, beautiful lady from a picture book; to others she can seem cold and pitiless. But before the second marriage she gives her lover the handkerchief stained in her dead husband's blood and she reveals that the self-subjugation which she will try to make of her new union will be a penance for her guilt and a protection against her own nature. To her first husband she was a beautiful siren to fight for; to her second she is a lovely ornament. Except for Waring's friendship her life will continue to be one of loneliness.

Not entirely unlike Bhanavar is Anna von Lenkenstein in *Vittoria,* whose beauty has made the gallant Weisspriess its victim. To possess the love of a daring soldier, the victor in duels, is a satisfaction to her haughty pride. But his grave illness brings to light her desperate need to love, and his later death leaves her with nothing to turn to for comfort. There are hints too of Bhanavar in Julia Rippenger, who for a while encourages the gallantry of Heriot to the near destruction of her husband's mind.

In each of his last three novels variations of Bhanavar appear. In *One of Our Conquerors* Judith Marsett, not yet twenty-three years of age, has already gone through the earlier stages and has reached that of mingled bitterness against men and desire for atonement. From obscure hints we gather that she has been an adventuress, and she still likes "love, blood, and adventure." Smartly dressed and usually well poised, she can lapse into the "Thames-water English of commerce and drainage" and into unrestrained outbursts of anger and self-condemnation. Her past and her unmarried position expose her to rudeness till she would be glad to murder. But there is penitence mixed with her desire to evade the past and to gain respectability as a captain's wife. She blames the corrupt teachings of a bard who is obviously Byron, and she speaks with hatred of men; but she is now desperately in love with her Ned. The story provides a happy though not inevitable denouement when Ned is sobered into a sense of integrity and marries her. Like other women in the novel, she joins collective woman in speaking of "bad women" and in hoping to shield any daughter of her own from knowledge of their ways.

In *Lord Ormont and His Aminta* it is Amy May whose life dangerously approaches that of the early Mrs. Lovell. Her husband has several times defended her honor, and he finally kills a man and flees the country. She has known of his previous duels in advance, but the last occurs without her knowledge. Meredith draws upon his store of metaphors to describe Amy's beauty:

> Her hair was radiant in a shady street; her eyelids tenderly toned around the almond enclosure of blue pebbles, bright as if shining from the seawash.

He adds that she is now using art to help nature defeat time. Of her fatal destiny he writes, "In the days when duelling flourished on our land, frail women could be powerful." Mrs. May does not comment on her fate; instead she pretends a calm assurance about her husband, whom she likes but does not love, and assumes her urbane role at a dinner party. But since even Ormont is said to praise yet not respect her, we are to conclude that her life is becoming steadily more desolate and that her husband's silence before the last duel forebodes trouble. Like Bhanavar she has been in lonely possession of love, revenge, and power, and according to Meredith's view nature benignly decrees that such persons "shall suffer."

Livia Fleetwood of *The Amazing Marriage* is also a winningly beautiful temptress. The unsophisticated Woodseer thinks of her as "a most heavenly lady, composed of day and night in her colouring, but more of night, where the western edge has become a pale steel blade." Wedded young to a man with a son her own age, she is a foot-loose, bored, and indeed corrupt widow, who gambles from ennui and finds amusement in watching the passions of the gamblers around her. She gives Woodseer money for play and seems almost the incarnation of Fortune, "the Black Goddess," who presides over the tables. Later a suicide is attributed to an infatuation for her; she can speak of love in woman as "lunacy and suicide." Little more than the ward of her son-in-law, Fleetwood, she hates him as a tyrant whom she must cajole and as a corrupter of men and women. The one person she deeply loves is the still-boyish and morally unstable Cressett, whom she tries vainly to protect from Fleetwood's encouragement to gamble and, after she has married him, from Fleetwood's and Feltre's persuasion to become a monk. Livia is sometimes kind, but life is mainly a frigid plateau for her; and her new marriage, her third, though it is rumored to have cured her of gambling, will not alter her loneliness.

All these women, whatever their sinister destinies, are alike in being the sterile products of a civilization that denies woman a useful career. Not that Meredith ignores character; even Judith would not blame all on fate. But they live an ornamental existence, unable to find adventure in work and tempted to use their beauty and brains in an egocentric contest which becomes more and more trivial unless tragedy intervenes. Meredith found them fascinating to contemplate and he did not contaminate his portraits by sentimentalizing. Had he given the women central space in his novels he might have expanded their mental struggles. As it was, he sketched in major outlines the pathos of arid lives cut off from the springs of elemental nature.

There are in the novels a number of other women who, without the tragic passions of these frustrate souls, are none the less victims of unfulfilment, their natural longings having no chance of expression. Such is Clare, who silently worships Richard, the god of her childhood horizons, only to commit suicide when sacrificed by her mother to be the wife of a doddering fool. Another is Juliana Bonner, rich but plain, who dies nursing an unrequited devotion to Evan. Much more charming in personality, with her classic beauty, is the pathetic Caroline, Evan's sister, married to the wife-beater Strike and in danger, from desperate loneliness, of seduction by a duke. In *Sandra Belloni* there is the unhappy Lady Charlotte, the twenty-nine-year-old ninth daughter of a "poor marquis." Were she a man, she believes, she could do heroic deeds. Instead she wastes her years in hunting and occasional social intrigue. She is "not a fascinating person," yet circumstances deny her any career except marriage. She offers in vain to share poverty with Wilfrid, and as Meredith tells us early that she has never really lived, we see no possibility of her ever escaping from the barren idleness to which rank unaccompanied by wealth or beauty commits her.

The loneliness of unwanted women, married to unappreciative dullards or languishing in unmarried fatuousness, was virtually an obsession of Meredith's. Besides such striking examples as Renée and Aminta and Harry Richmond's Aunt Dorothy, there are Lady Blandish, Mrs. Warder-Devereux, Mrs. Jacob Blathenoy, and others, some of them characterized only by reference to their melancholy. They all live out their lives in anxiety or bleakness unless a Weyburn or a Lydiard offers rescue. Such portraits serve usually to fill a small section of the complex pattern in a Meredithian novel. The accounts may be intense, as in Renée's rejection by Beauchamp or the diary of Clare. The sketches, however, are primarily lyric rather than dramatic studies of conflict and development.

Much more dramatic and consequently vaster in range are the tragic conflicts in *Rhoda Fleming, The Tale of Chloe,* and *Diana of the Crossways.* Though Mrs. Lovell is the most interesting woman in *Rhoda Fleming,* the central theme concerns Rhoda and Dahlia Fleming as the chief embodiments of the forces at war in human nature.

Like the later Diana, the heroines live on after what would normally be the tragic conclusion. Dahlia's seven-year survival of her attempted suicide is in its saintliness in accord with a tragic ending; but Rhoda's contented marriage after she has ignorantly done great evil is anticlimactic. Meredith may have provided such a conclusion because in life itself a Rhoda would outlast sorrow and, with mild atonement, regain her former assurance. We are confronted, however, with the feeling that a more traditional denouement would better have expressed the tragedy inherent in her spiritual civil war. We feel too that the excellent characterizations of Edward Blancove and of Mrs. Lovell are at the expense of interest in Rhoda, whom the novelist seemed glad to dismiss from the scene. Yet in the contrasts of values—for though Meredith does not tell us to, we are to regard each of the other characters in reference to Rhoda—the author was dealing in the elemental substance of tragedy.

As there is nothing in the appearance or the commonly accepted meanings of the flowers to account for Meredith's choice of names, he may have intended the names of both girls to express their mother's wish to make a flower garden in escape from the otherwise austere farm existence which contented her husband. The novelist stresses the opposition in temperament of the parents, and also their cardinal defects. Mrs. Fleming is not practical; her unimaginative husband is especially unappreciative of flowers and all the intangibles which they suggest. Both the daughters are the victims of their parents' limitations. They are meant to typify generic weaknesses in a civilization which, by making a separation between duty and toil, on the one hand, and beauty and enjoyment, on the other, sets man at war with himself and leaves him no touchstone of conduct.

In the few pages given to the portrait of Mrs. Fleming, who dies at the beginning of the novel, Meredith has sketched a subdued expression of the essential traits of the Great Mel. She cultivates poppies—weeds, Fleming calls them—while in debt to the grocer. She educates her daughters superficially in the social graces and gives them an illusion of the glamorous life of high society. Like the generations of girls before them, Rhoda and Dahlia read courtly French romances and such stories as that of the Queen of Sheba. They dream of London and imitate the dress of the rector's wife. By the beauty and elegant grace of Mrs. Lovell, who appears one day in church, they are completely entranced.

Fleming's contribution is summed up in his self-satisfied comment that he has not required the girls to do too much housework and that they have been taught to sew and to say their prayers. His brother-in-law later remarks that he attends "Methody meetins and quotes Scriptur." He is a hard puritan, unable to sympathize with others and defining duty in unimaginative terms. Each of his daughters must be made secure in life by marriage. He would wed Rhoda to the old farm worker Gammon or to the worthless Algernon rather than see her unprotected. When Dahlia has been seduced he asks only that she be made respectable, no matter what kind of man becomes her husband. He is, in short, Scott's Davie Deans without that soul-searching humanity that ennobled Davie.

We are not told whether in permitting his wife to grow flowers and engage in little extravagances Fleming has a secret envy of her attitude; but we do know that Rhoda has an intense conflict of mind because she loves Dahlia, who is like her mother, yet must, like Fleming, condemn her. Fleming is too unsuccessful and too petty in his hardness to be a tragic tyrant. He merely represents mediocre human nature shutting out beauty and adventure and adhering rigorously to convention in order to have a limited mental security. His married life has given not a true affinity but rather a compromise of two souls, with each enduring the weakness of the other. The novelist's idealism, however, required something very different from compromise—a transcendence, in which there would be no conflict between duty and the desire to enjoy. His story of Rhoda and Dahlia is concerned with the initial conflict, especially in Rhoda, with the temptation to let duty triumph or else to settle for a truce, and with the ultimate transcendence, which is achieved fully by Dahlia and to a degree by Rhoda.

The seduction of Dahlia by Edward Blancove is no malicious deception of a trusting girl by a villain. It is the end toward which Dahlia's temperament and artificial education naturally lead. She has an idyllic concept of the life of upper society and of the chivalric perfection of its young heroes, and she finds distasteful the ugliness of what is to her exile from romance in her father's home. What she learns is not hatred for Edward but disillusionment. And when she has suffered the bitterness of awaking, she has to undergo, besides, all the cruel punishment inflicted by the puritanism from which she has fled. She cries out against her sister and her father, and her attempt at suicide is a climactic rebellion against their inexorable wills. In the purification of mind which accompanies convalescence Dahlia realizes that neither the things which she dreamed nor the actual desolate life which disillusion has revealed are of ultimate consequence. Without retreating to a convent she comes to accept a saint-like detachment from worldly struggle. Her mother's flight from harsh reality and her father's dour insensibility are alike trivial when contrasted with her transcendence of both. As one follows her history he is immersed in the question, why does nature decree that a beautiful unselfish girl shall suffer? The answer is typical of tragedy, for through suffering Dahlia reaches a calmness of mind with "all passion spent."

The personality of Rhoda is more complex than Dahlia's. Although Stevenson admired her, her portrait is not one to inspire unmixed sympathy. Meredith is successful in showing her hardness and ignorance, but he often has to resort to exposition to argue that she should be pitied for them. Instead of showing us in step-by-step detail how home training and the general moral environment tend to stifle her better feelings, he presents her at the end of the process, when the injury has been done and Rhoda is the unsympathetic result. We perceive that hers is a character in which many impulses are struggling below the conscious surface, and we feel that the author has scanted the exploration of their causes.

The portrait which he gives is a study in self-repression. Younger than Dahlia, Rhoda is handsome rather than pretty; the servant calls her a "tiger girl." She does have strong feminine impulses, and she unconsciously envies Dahlia for the romantic life which she ignorantly imagines her to have in her uncle's London home. The author comments, "As the sun is wanted to glorify the right features of a landscape, this girl thirsted for a dose of golden flattery." But the hard outlines of her face and her haughty pride show how determinedly her impulses have been throttled. Rhoda has indeed a fear of her own nature. Meredith once likens her to an Old Testament heroine; since she sees ethics mainly as conformity to convention and her father's teaching, her courage and zeal presuppose a wrathful Jehovah, whose negative commandments she must obey. When Dahlia has sinned, Rhoda is so obsessed with the sin that she magnifies the shame and makes it her own. Because she herself would pay any price to destroy it she expects Dahlia to atone by marrying whoever will wed her, and she actually wishes that the girl had died.

What makes Rhoda so tigerish in her determination is that she must keep prisoner the rebel in her own nature. In becoming a conscience for another she is a reincarnation of a Grand Inquisitor burning a heretic to protect a faith which questioning might destroy. Meredith himself considers Dahlia's folly an evil thing, but her inevitable suffering is heavy payment. In Rhoda he presents the distortion that results when, forgetting that error brings its own natural punishment, one imposes a penalty which is unnatural and arbitrary.

The reversal that must occur is, of course, that Rhoda shall see her own sin and feel remorse for what she has done. Meredith brings this about only after she has several times seen a glimpse of the truth but, following a lifetime habit, has shut it out as an illusion. When she does begin to see that pride is mixed in with her harshness she is about to relent, but even then she wishes that her lover would impetuously settle all qualms of conscience for her. Instead, like Meredith's other lover-friends, he merely gives her encouragement and she has to make her own decision that she has erred and to pay a heavier price in atonement than she expected him to assess.

To this point the novel follows a tragic sequence for Rhoda, but whereas in the usual tragedy her discovery would lead only to penance, Meredith has intended from the beginning to have her recover to enjoy the springtime which she has so far missed.

Her relations with Robert would be pointless if she were not ultimately to unfold her frustrated nature as his wife. She is both a tragic protagonist, whose recognition of her error gives the reader a katharsis, and a resilient heroine, who shares with the reader in benefiting from what she has learned and building a new life upon it. In accord with the author's thesis the hard lines of her character become softened, and though she will not be a paragon of understanding, her married life will be much richer than her inhibited youth. Yet what she has done is a terrible deed, even though she is a product of mankind's composite folly. If it be granted that a traditional denouement with a tragic ending for Rhoda would have taken little skill to arrange, it is also true that neither Meredith's ingenuity nor his shrewd development of a thesis compensates for the anticlimax.[23]

There are diverse tones in the short *Tale of Chloe,* 1879, but there is a much better artistic fusion than in *Rhoda Fleming.* Beamish, as the disillusioned dictator of Bath, personifies discretion attempting to impose civilized conduct on mankind while accepting as inevitable the vagaries of human nature. He recommends to the Duke of Dewlap that the young duchess be allowed £1000 to lose at gambling, but he jerks false lace from her attire and he otherwise demands of his subjects absolute submission to his standards of decorum. Apart from the medium which he provides for satiric aspersions on English conduct, he establishes an atmosphere in which the protagonist moves with the appearance of serenity while masking the anguish of her heart. Beamish knows that Chloe is unhappy and he respects her for the disciplined disguise of her feelings. It is her adherence to Beamish's principles that gives her tragedy its emotional compression. Her strongest gesture of grief upon each of her lover's infidelities has been the tying of another knot in a silken cord.

The Duchess of Dewlap, unformed, even vulgar in manner, is at the other extreme of human nature from Beamish. She has no discretion, no intellectual restraint. She simply wants to be happy: "I've a real lark going on in me all day long." Married to a "duke instead of a husband," she welcomes flattery and would naïvely elope with Chloe's worthless betrayer. In describing her Meredith has assumed an air of playful romance, telling with poetic flourishes of the courtship of duke and country girl, a subject dear to pastoral story but to comedy as well. The novelist's version leaves the duchess unsophisticated and helpless in an artificial world. The duke can provide nothing but conventional dullness, and despite his allowing her the brief excitement of gambling, Beamish offers mainly a negative discipline of restraint. The duchess is the raw material of life. Not immoral and not consciously selfish, she wants to live abundantly and cannot understand why the circumstantial will should ever say, "Thou shalt not."

In Beamish and the duchess we have respectively intellect and blood, the first two in Meredith's trinity. In Chloe these have been transcended by spirit, for Chloe has known yet more intensely than the country girl the wild pulsing of blood. Indeed it is because she wants to keep her returned lover near her yet a day or two that she actually risks his seducing the young wife. But she has too the power of disillusioned reflection, which tells her that her lover is false and that refusal to accept that fact means sacrificing another. Her suicide to warn the foolish duchess is the supreme expression of spirit. This time Meredith does not settle for less than the art demands. Chloe's death brings to Beamish and the duchess and indeed to the sentimental, irresponsible lover a sudden awareness of something altogether nobler than their own lives.

When the novelist came to the writing of *Diana of the Crossways,* published in 1885, he had already been experimenting with tragicomedy and he was also much concerned with the subjugation of women. His attempt to exemplify his thesis led him to coerce the plot into a pattern to express his theme. In its simplest aspect Diana's story is of a woman's being shocked in her search for masculine companionship, of her consequent struggle to achieve Amazonian independence, with the inevitable disaster to which her inexperience must lead, and of her recognizing finally that the companionship which she once sought is possible.

So stated, the plot permits a conflict and reversal. In actuality, however, Meredith was interested primarily in the first part, in which Diana seeks love and yet recalls a sharply bitter past, with various men figuring in her memory as hounds eager for the chase. Her dilemma he recognized as deeply fixed in her nature, though unfortunately he did not dramatize her semiconsciousness to reveal the images and half-articulate concepts which make her afraid. Indeed the shocks are presented either by external action or by the briefest second-hand report: "Her experience had awakened a sexual aversion, of some slight kind, enough to make her feminine pride stipulate for perfect independence, that she might have the calm out of which imagination spreads wing." One incident obliquely referred to in chapter four is evidently the same as that again ambiguously and belatedly discussed in chapter forty-one, in which the boastful liar Wroxeter is revealed as having been one of the rude offenders. A major shock, which she later blames for her foolish marriage, is the attempt at an embrace by her best friend's philandering husband, a comic sensualist. These are the wounds which cause Diana to marry for self-protection; and her husband, who scarcely appears in the novel, intensifies them by his crude, unsympathetic tyranny. The premarital incidents might conceivably be grave enough to bring terror to a girl who can idolize Platonically an elderly general and can later defy the world's wife by again Platonically loving an elderly statesman. But since in *The Tragic Comedians* and in *One of Our Conquerors* the novelist did briefly explore semiconscious images, the superficial sketch of Diana's fears is singular. Meredith's letters reveal that he was physically tired when he was working on the novel and that he had no great enthusiasm for the story.

Where he was most inventive was in picturing the giddiness to which the wounds have led. Diana is beautiful, but she has little interest in her feminine charm. In her retreat from emotion she is determined to live on an intellectual plane, and in time her drawing room becomes a jousting place for tilting wits, with Diana the blue-stocking queen. In her less thoughtful moments she is hard and brittle, and she lives in a milieu where neither women nor men express more than the superficial aspects of their intellects. A sudden act of gentleness from time to time reminds us how artificial is Diana's cultivated manner and how pathetic therefore the perversion from nature.

According to the author the cause of the tragedy, as with Rhoda, is in civilization itself. Collective mankind demands that the individual upper-class woman conform to a pattern which denies the existence of blood and requires the disguise of intellect, pretending that woman is pure soul. The woman who attempts to escape has only a wilderness before her. In asserting that Diana is to be admired for being unlike the candle-worshiping Constance Asper and all who represent the world's wife, Meredith emphatically puts the initial blame on society, not on his heroine, who has had no fair choice. But whereas in portraying Rhoda he never laughed at her tragic error, he at times turns the comic imps loose upon Diana. If the Constances lack depth of soul because of the denial of their human impulses and talents, the earthly devotees of the goddess Diana also live but partial lives. With her bitter experience as the cause, Meredith's heroine is comic in renouncing blood to live as sheer intellect, with herself the cynosure for lovers of mental brilliance. The novelist dramatizes Diana's sparkling wit fests, but the denouement reveals her folly.

Having laughed with and at Diana, the novelist swung abruptly back to stress her innate tenderness and to show the pathos of her artificial life. She would be courageous, yet her consent, as a married woman, to elope with Dacier, whom she has idealized, is not a confident embarkation such as Aminta's was to be, but an anxious, indeed sinful act of running away; and when the illness of her friend, Lady Dunstane, jolts her into awareness she sees the elopement as a temptation escaped. The experience is unfortunately a major crisis which causes her to shrink to a tragic degree from all that is symbolized by blood.

Though in a way the climax has been prepared for, it comes with a swift suddenness. To win a kiss from Diana, now a widow, Dacier returns late at night and confides a secret of state. In mad confusion, shamed by his advance, harassed by the need of money, and humiliated because a newspaper editor has sneered at her knowledge of politics, in which she has hoped to be initiate, Diana rushes to the editor with the story. Meredith may have started his work on the novel with this scene in mind, for he was influenced by the erroneous report of Mrs. Norton's betrayal of a state secret, and his novel had to progress to an act of folly which would bring with it a cure.

The betrayal, however, is unconvincing. Arguments defending it insist that such an act is true to life, but this fact still does not make it true for Diana or significant for the reader.[24] Had Mrs. Norton actually been guilty, Meredith would yet have had to imagine the motivation which would inspire the deed, and the reader would want to immerse himself in Diana's thoughts, emotions, and physical sensations for the incident to become artistically important. Instead there is an unusual lack of mental analysis. We see Diana almost entirely from without, and her actions are only a very general indication of her confusion. The novelist asserts the confusion instead of revealing its special nature. While recognizing that the idea of betrayal may be plausible, one should admit that the execution of the scene is wanting, and execution is indispensable in art.

With the evil committed, Diana has the calm that follows exhaustion. Later she protests to Dacier that she had no notion that she was doing wrong, and though Meredith dramatizes her inconsistency as she stammers out her defense, he still does not clarify her action. When much later he says that even Lady Dunstane was never to understand, though she did not blame Diana, he tacitly admits that he himself accepts the deed as beyond psychological representation. When after Dacier's rejection of her—which includes his burning unopened a voluminous letter of explanation whose contents we are forced to surmise—Diana undergoes a nervous breakdown, she condemns her foolish life, including the betrayal; yet she still seems to think Dacier unfair. More to the point, Meredith throws the blame largely on Dacier for impelling the act and he damns him for not having compassion, as if his obtuseness somehow lightened Diana's guilt.

In a letter written while he was completing the novel Meredith protested, lightly yet with exasperation, that he could gladly kill Diana and conclude her story.[25] It was not necessary, to be sure, that she should die, but after physical recovery she might have been allowed a subdued life of renunciation. She is guilty—this she recognizes—but since, with the author's approval, she still complains against fate, she is not fully resigned. Though she has been led astray from a natural simplicity, Meredith will not sacrifice her as a victim of an artificial civilization. For a good tragedy he might well have abandoned the half-facetious tone with which, for example, he made her financial distress a humorous personification of male debit versus female credit, and he should have shown how at the moment when Dacier affronts her Diana's mind is a mad whirl of impulses and apprehensions. Initial blame could still be on the world to which the conventional Dacier belongs, but Diana could be the perverted result. Then the action of betrayal would be plausible and artistically valid as a climax and the denouement could be brief. With self-discovery and a sense of lasting shame which would arouse our pity as her and Meredith's defense do not, Diana would remain the tragic representation of the waste which civilization permits.

The novelist was so determined, however, to give not only warning but guidance, that he would not stop with the tragic portrayal of a woman's losing what nature meant her to have. Realizing that nothing which could follow the catastrophe could equal it in interest, he entitled the subsequent action an "anticlimax," as if to say that the reader must break free from traditional novelistic forms and accept the label as irony. Then he took Diana, in the general pattern of Beauchamp's career —and of the later Aminta's—through a delayed youth in which, with the ever-faithful Redworth, she finds delight in elemental country life and is prepared at the end to answer with a sentimental, one might say Victorian, twitch of her fingers an allusion to a baby.

Because Diana must, in this aftermath, learn anew, Meredith could purge her only of certain major faults, and could not let tragedy achieve absolute purification. As she starts afresh she must still have a sharp tongue and retain her earlier suspicions of men, for she is now a romantic heroine beginning a new quest. In the scenes that complete the novel she does not become perfect, but in the manner of those other romantics—Evan, Harry, Beauchamp—she attains to a greater sanity. The aftermath is, however, not only an anticlimax, but a new story. The character in whom we have been interested is the Diana who has fought courageously and alone, who has consequently made a tragic error and should be purified entirely by suffering. Romance, as in *The Ordeal,* may give way to tragedy, but tragedy cannot yield to romance.

One can only wish that a novelist who so well understood nature's decree that erring mortals must suffer had written full-length narratives about two or three of the minor characters—they are all women—whose tragic lives we have reviewed. One could wish too that instead of trying to provide additional instruction by means of Rhoda's and Diana's married careers he had built his stories to a simple tragic climax and stopped.

Chapter Eight

Richard Feverel's Tragic Ordeal

You burly lovers on the village green,
Yours is a lower, and a happier star!
(Modern Love)

WHEN Meredith began *The Ordeal of Richard Feverel,* he had behind him *The Shaving of Shagpat* and *Farina* and the 1851 edition of *Love in the Valley,* all three rarefied distillations of life in the manner of allegory and pastoral. The characters and the incidents were derived from reality and were translatable again into actual life, but they were clothed in the metaphor of poetic romance. He was now concerned to give his fiction a local habitation, to show human passion at play in nineteenth-century English settings. In *The Ordeal* he achieved some of his finest scenes of pathos and tragedy.

The novelist was still, however, very much interested in tracing the design, as one might in a tapestry, and in making it conspicuous amid the multiplicity of detail. His propensity for outlining the pattern and giving comic designations to its features was to remain with him throughout his writing career. It was especially apparent, however, in the first, 1859, version of *The Ordeal;* and though in revising he excised many of the more farcical elements, his final, 1875, version begins with a comic framework, retains comic terminology while moving through pastoral romance, and is loath, indeed too loath, to relinquish its witty commentary as the narrative plunges toward its tragic end.

To stress the fact that, despite its peculiar variations, what happened to an English family in the nineteenth century was as generic as anything in the history of Shibli or Bhanavar or of Farina and the Cologne monk, the author repeatedly inserted allegorical labels. Most prominent, as the title itself indicates, is the concept of Feverel life as an ordeal. Though the novel is to conclude as the tragedy of Richard, the first version begins in a tone even lighter than that used later to introduce Sir Willoughby's comedy. Each of various Feverels is facetiously caricatured as the victim of Mrs. Malediction, and Sir Caradoc has emphasized a "special Ordeal" as the distinguishing characteristic of Feverel fate. Sir Austin sentimentaliy regards his wife's desertion as his ordeal and enjoys having been considered worthy of persecution by the "Fates and Furies." Losing of a leg in a cricket match and suffering from dyspepsia are variant manifestations of the ordeal.

Still in a light vein comes the introduction of Richard and, by way of "The Pilgrim's Scrip," the label which superficially indicates his ordeal. The Pilgrim's Scrip is a complex improvement upon the choral rhymes in *The Shaving of Shagpat.* Written by the pseudo-wise Sir Austin, it contains many aphorisms which imply shrewd sense, for the sentimenalist, Meredith liked to point out, can speak aptly against the very sin which he commits. But it also has cynical worldly wisdom expressive of Sir Austin's pique against the woman who left him for a worthless rhymester. It is the Wise Youth who, seeing clearly another's sins though never his own, christens the Scrip "The Great Shaddock Dogma"—shaddock, or grapefruit, being understood by those who are clever to be the forbidden fruit to which Eve introduced Adam in Eden. Before Richard has dreamed of love Sir Austin has written with bitterness of what Meredith here and again later calls the "Apple-Disease." With further involvement of the metaphor, the novelist says (in a passage deleted in the revised version) that Sir Austin plans to guard Richard "like a Tree of Eden; by advancing him to a certain moral fortitude ere the Apple-Disease was spontaneously developed, there would be seen something approaching to a perfect Man." Thus before the lad starts on his career the novelist has designated the paternal interference which will create his *ordeal.* Near the end the term is again to become prominent when Adrian in specific allusion to the malediction of Sir Austin's Shaddock Dogma, once quips, "O Richard of the Ordeal!"

In a manner strongly reminiscent of *The Shaving of Shagpat,* others besides Richard and the Wise Youth are characterized under the terms of comedy or allegorical romance. Benson, the butler, who protects Sir Austin during the siege by female admirers, is both "the Great Shaddock Dogma condensed in a look" and the "Saurian": "As Dragons of old guarded the dwellings of beautiful princesses, Heavy Benson stood sentinel over the Baronet." (This passage too was deleted.) The dissipated old sinner Hippias, who glamorizes his illness as his ordeal, is simply "the Dyspepsy." Sir Miles Papworth, candidate for Parliament, is two circles set upon stumps. There are scores of caricatured women who, with a motherly tenderness that does not preclude marriage, idolize Sir Austin for what they believe is sweetness concealed within the acerbity of his Scrip. Particularly there is Mrs. Grandison, a caricature of misguided mothers and of all the female descendants of Sir Charles.

The labels and motifs extend to the personification of attitudes. In a dialogue of Sir Austin and Richard, for example, the two are "Cold Blood" and "Hot Blood." Once when Sir Austin is debating with himself the negative arguments are spoken by the devil. Simplicity in feeling as contrasted with sophistication is a manifestation of nature personified; the change that takes place in Richard when he walks in the German forest comes under the chapter title "Nature Speaks." A rather arbitrary symbol is the cypress, which for the young lovers is always, as might be expected, a foreboding of ill.

Significant too are the allusions to literature, especially to Shakespeare and to classical comedy. In "Ferdinand and Miranda" the novelist indicates the standard his readers are to accept in reading his great love scene. For a commentary on the wooing of Richard by Bella, after a scene reminiscent of *Faust,* he rephrases the famous lines in *Richard III,* giving to his Richard the lady's role: "Was ever hero in this fashion won?" The first reference to "the new Comedy" (later deleted) is without a capital *n,* and the term describes what the unlettered Tom Bakewell feels engaged in. The second, with a capital, refers to Ripton's anticipation of an adventure involving lover, beloved, and disapproving father, an adventure, in short, suggestive of Terence and of what Meredith knew of Menander. Again, a chapter title includes "the Last Act of the Comedy." A reference also to Sir Austin as having been "the God of the machine" admits a parallel that Meredith certainly recognized between the denouement of his tragedy and Greek drama.

Most of these allegorical designations and commentaries were retained in the final draft of the novel, but their total was substantially—though still not sufficiently—reduced in frequency and form. The caricatures, including those of the besieging ladies, were either stricken out entirely or compressed to passing allusions. An entire chapter on Sir Austin's visit to Mrs. Grandison was omitted, and with it scattered paragraphs elsewhere referring to the Grandisons and the paragon Sir Charles. The excised passages, which are mainly in the opening scenes, indicate the transitional nature of *The Ordeal.* The novelist could not determine what attitude to take toward his characters and theme, and the story altered as he wrote. When he began to enter deeply into the conflict in Sir Austin's mind and into the passions of Richard he must have perceived that his apparatus tended to reduce his characters to superficial comic types. The most striking evidence of Meredith's increasing depth within the first version itself is the fact that Richard's tragedy develops into something much more serious than Adrian's quip implies; so that the very word *ordeal* as employed by the Wise Youth is an ironic understatement of an experience which, far from being peculiar to a fated few, symbolizes the eternally repeated process of man's coming spiritually of age. Entertaining though the light comedy is, it represents no advance over Meredith's earlier work. It is only when the tragedy becomes ominous that the wittiness develops depth and the elements fuse into a unified story.

For Richard the tragic denouement is the more intense because it springs from and contrasts with romance. In a pastoral world—and Meredith liked to contemplate such an ideal realm—the young heroes lead wholesome lives. They may suffer love sickness, even jealousy, and, as in *Sandra Belloni,* they may break heads in open but transitory wrath. They may have to war against evil, and they will endure the natural, inevitable sorrow of a Moschus for Bion. But there is no place for an ordeal. The pastoral is an unreal world, of course, to the extent that the heroes are free of life's petty frustrations and their spiritual problems are reducible to order. But though in this sense unreal, the pastoral is the norm by which to judge actual human error. No more than Milton could Meredith dispense with a garden of Eden.

Richard Feverel begins his career therefore, not as a burly lover on the village green, to be sure, but as a romantic boy for whom a pastoral sequence would seem appropriate. The poaching, the rick burning, and, as a climax to all, the discovery of Lucy by the stream are adventures which belong in a serpentless meadow. But though Richard has not yet tasted of the knowledge of good and evil, there is guarding him a saurian, Sir Austin, who, having found the shaddock bitter, believes Eden itself to be inherently satanic. Nature to Sir Austin is indiscriminately rank, breeding riotously and recklessly wasting; man must protect himself against its licentious extravagance, and his duty extends to the careful watching of others, who must not be allowed to eat of the shaddock until they are mature, yet must miraculously accept the wisdom of one who has eaten.

Sir Austin is so replete with contradictions that it is impossible to decide at times whether to blame more his theory of education or his frequent violations of it. Like the later Sir Willoughby he has contempt for poetry and glorifies what he believes is science. In the name of science he exposes Richard to the vice of London, convinced that he is thus gradually bringing the boy to readiness for the apple. He stresses the scientific impersonality with which he withholds forgiveness from Richard when he is actually avenging his own wounded pride.[26] In the belief that nature must be followed he expects Lucy to nurse her baby when she is ill, and in disregard for nature, he reproaches her though she is mentally distraught. His essential sin, however, from which the lesser evils spring, is sentimental egoism. Having tasted of the gall of the Roc, he has lost all appetite for adventure and become defensive. He will risk nothing lest he lose again, and instead jealously guards his one possession, the son whom his deserting wife has left him. Richard must belong to him completely; there is no place for Clare and none for Lucy unless she will belong to him too and serve his purpose with Richard. He will shut out the world from the castle where he has imprisoned Richard and will take the youth on what he believes are guarded tours outside the walls to prove why he should return within.

At one level Sir Austin's folly exemplifies the erring of civilization when it denies the natural coursing of the blood and becomes a negation of adventure; this, as we have seen, Meredith was consistently to deplore in nineteenth-century England. More profoundly, it is a study of the ubiquitous tendency toward the supreme evil, the desire to possess another's soul and to act for it the part of a god.

Another form of evil is meant to be typified by the cynic Adrian. In the 1859 edition Adrian's sensual indulgence with a servant girl is explicit, and his hypocritical pretense is ridiculed by the girl. When revising, Meredith struck out the reference to licentiousness in the comic bucolic dialogue, and he otherwise trimmed the sketch of Adrian, still depicting him as a callous sensualist, but stressing rather his disbelief in human goodness and his assumption that living is primarily a game of intrigue. Body and intellect are divorced in him except as intellect provides plans for bodily indulgence. Wit is for Adrian a refuge against the intrusion of any moral or emotional consideration. Like other minor characters in Meredith's works, the Wise Youth is worthy of a larger portrait, for he is essentially a miniature of Mephistopheles as wit. His vanity is ludicrous, especially when he believes that his sophisticated manner will win Lucy's admiration. Yet laughable though he is, Adrian is a satanic imp. His example in cynicism is harmful to the impressionable Richard, and his advice, which ignores human longings, helps prevent reconciliation of father and son.

Not all the minor exemplifications of folly have an important effect on Richard's life, but they do fill in a background of egoism and error. Such are the ordeal-suffering Algernon and Hippias, the unfaithful Berry, Mrs. Grandison, and the feckless Sandoe. Pure sensuality, on the other hand, in the form of Lord Mountfalcon, is of major importance both as a touchstone by which to judge Richard and as the immediate cause of the catastrophe. As we saw in chapter three, Mountfalcon is utterly comic. He is as obedient as any Ovidian seducer to Lucy's will, but instead of being rewarded with physical tokens of compassion, he is subjected to tedious instruction in virtue. To keep the sensuality of Mountfalcon dominant Meredith avoided giving him all the other wickedness which a villain might show; when, for example, he is challenged by Richard, he is indeed coerced into taking part in the nonsensical duel. As a sensualist Mountfalcon is not only a cause of evil to others; he is himself as unfortunate as the later Algernon Blancove. Desiring only pleasure, he is actually wretched; and indolent by nature, he is feverishly occupied.

It is in the world represented by these secondary characters that Richard's personality and his ordeal take on meaning. Because it is meant to be inclusive the life of Richard shows resemblances to the lives of various minor characters who are merely personifications of one or another attitude. Its most tragic errors parallel those of Sir Austin, Adrian, and Mountfalcon. Like his father, Richard is at times possessed by egoism, especially in his thoughtless cruelty to Clare and to Lucy. He is the victim of Mephistophelean doubt, which he cannot dismiss with the Wise Youth's urbane dispassion. And he plunges into sensuality, from which, unlike Mountfalcon, he recoils with tragicomic revulsion.

It is because he lives in a world where he is surrounded by unpropitious examples—for he has learned even of sensuality long before meeting Mountfalcon or Bella—that the youth finds encouragement to err. The direction of his folly is very much determined by the meddling of his father. When in the rick-burning affair Sir Austin undermines his heroism by secret intrigue, a breach begins; with the destruction of his poetry it becomes too wide for bridging. Richard is left with suspicion of his father, whom he would love if he could, and so he learns none of the wisdom which was intended to see him safely through the apple-disease. In a limited sense his ordeal is that he must spend most of his life from early adolescence onward as a victim of the disease, for disease it is for Richard.

He is dominated by preoccupation with women; indeed he has no other career. And yet he comes to each new situation in helpless ignorance. Shut out as he is from knowledge of the actual natures of women, he creates idealized abstractions; and his tragedy stems from his not seeing the inferiority of the idealizations to the realities themselves.

When Richard is seven years old he wakes to find a lady bending over his bed. As she is his mother, the action becomes symbolic of her shadow upon his soul. There is an unspoken feeling in Richard that sinister things have occurred, and in the light of what happens later it is clear that he suspects his father of being to blame. When he does finally rescue his mother the young man is so involved in new perplexities with Lucy and Bella that Meredith scants the incident, leaving obscure the effect upon Richard himself. The quest for a mother is shown to have been as deeply inspired, however, as the longing for a father's understanding, and yet Lady Feverel has been for Richard an idealized lonely sufferer untouched by commonplace actuality.

It is sight of Lady Blandish's bonnet that causes the boy to lose his swimming match, and it is overhearing what Richard —and she too for a while—thinks is Sir Austin's wooing of her that gives him notions on courtship. She is just enough removed from him to allow chivalric transformation; she might as easily be a lady in a book of fashions, for the lad never thinks of her as a pathetic and subtly perceptive woman.

There is, of course, the natural adolescent dreaming of ideal loves, and it is from this that Richard is suddenly transported to a yet more intense dream of Lucy. The Ferdinand-Miranda relationship is for Meredith as for Shakespeare of enchanting beauty. He would not have Richard at once bound to earth by practical considerations. But whereas Lucy can be idealistic and practical too, Richard has no understanding of her as a person. Clare has been taken from him, he has known no girls well, and he has only an imagined concept into which he tries to make Lucy fit.

In the first edition Carola Grandison, a young girl who wishes she were a boy, gains Richard's affection when he is confused by Lucy's being taken from him. The incident is plausible and it prepares for later defection after his marriage. The author may have cut it because he was eliminating the chapter on the Grandison family, or simply because, though believable, it came too early in his presentation of Richard's infidelity and could not be allowed interesting development. Significantly, when with Carola, Richard is utterly imperceptive; he likes her for her seeming boyishness and never appreciates the drama of rebellion within her mind.

It is after he has undiscerningly separated from Lucy and after a Thames holiday with women of uncertain character that Richard starts out to rescue lost women, who, he imagines, are waiting to be redeemed to virtue and security. But he once more sets up an idealization that keeps him from seeing the actual. Bella is a fallen soul, then she is a fascinating witch, and soon Richard thrills to the voluptuous thought that she and he are fated to be supremely wicked together and to join the damned in Hell. The real Bella is no saint, but unlike Richard she can fall in love, and it is too late before Richard awakens to the cruelty he has committed in ignorance of her true nature.

The death of Clare might well be the cilmax to a tragic hero's education, for Richard undergoes deep contrition of spirit when he reads Clare's diary. But he soon descends again into insane folly, from which he must be rescued anew. It was a conviction of Meredith that man and woman are not only not limited to one love, but in the struggle to find their own identities in the social universe are often unconsciously wasteful of the souls which love them. In this respect Clare is the victim of Richard's extravagance. As a girl she has been banished from his company by the barbarous egoism of Sir

Austin, and as a young woman she has been wedded to a dolt because her mother knew no alternative to marriage. In Clare as in Lucy, Meredith provides an ironic contrast to Richard. His career is meteoric, hers outwardly colorless and submissive to fate. And yet it is Clare whose passions have been unceasingly of heroic magnitude. The discovery of the truth can bring nothing but shame to Richard, because in his self-indulgent acceptance of Clare's devotion he has actually been toying with her very life.

Though the recognition that the real Clare was not a passionless, bloodless abstraction is like seeing a miracle for Richard, Meredith had not said all he wished of man's ordeal. Richard's thoughtless cruelty to Clare is the outgrowth of Sir Austin's egoistic attempt to keep him from loving her. But although as in Donne's poem we can add to the father's sins those which he has led Richard to sin, by the time of Clare's suicide Richard himself is blindly egoistic. Sobering as the shock is to him, he is still unable to see a living woman as he sees the dead one. There follows a friendly association with Judith Feltre, unhappily wedded to a "decrepit lord" and seeking distraction on the continent. But even when he wins sympathy from Judith, Richard never has more than a superficial awareness of her suffering. His thoughts are still fixed painfully upon himself.

The youth does come to pity Lucy and to yearn for forgiveness; but far from telling her the whole truth, he flees from her to commit yet another infidelity. For the duel itself is a disloyalty to Lucy and reveals how little Richard comprehends her love. The Richard who insists that Mountfalcon give him satisfaction is tragicomic. He has committed acts of which he is intensely ashamed, and he wants to regain integrity. Yet, like any sentimentalist, he does not want to pay an honest price. He dramatizes his guilt to Lucy, but he is still his own hero, determined to make circumstance, in the form of Mountfalcon, the villain. Lucy's virtue and reputation are unsullied; she has not been emotionally harmed by the attempt at seduction. Richard's seduction of Bella, on the other hand—for he actually wins her love rather than she his—is a very real tampering with another's soul; and the fact that Bella is ennobled by her love in no way mitigates Richard's guilt. Yet he will fight a duel as if destruction of a villain would remove all sin from himself and leave him freed from his past. He has suffered for his treatment of Clare, and during his walk in the German forest, including the finding and nursing of the leveret, he has sensed his cruelty to Lucy. Nevertheless it is only a finer abstraction than before from whom he asks forgiveness, while withholding the secret of his last, worst sin of all.

At the end, as in all tragedy, we see how far we have come. The eating of the shaddock is a symbol no longer limited to the apple sickness. Through his futile quest to find in Sir Austin a true father and through perceiving the anguish that he has caused—for Clare's and Lucy's deaths will forever weigh his spirit—he has come to the irrevocable knowledge of good and evil. Lucy's death is indeed the incident which signifies his irreparable loss of Eden. His few years have brought him not increased relish of good things, but the terrifying vision of his father's error and of his own. He does have one precious awareness which the Sir Austins of this world can never know. When dying, Lucy has cried out against the egoist's cold harshness, and Lady Blandish pictures him as a creature in Hell. Sir Austin's sensation is at best negative. He cannot feel the kind of shame that brings purification; he knows only bafflement and bitter loss. In contrast, though he has not found a father and though he will forever suffer remorse for his own guilt, Richard has as never before in his mind the image of Lucy, and in its essence it is now a true image. Like Othello, he sees finally how much better she was than any of his idealizations of woman.

From the vantage point of the tragic ending we can judge both the framework of the novel and the qualities which make the story significant. In the abstract concept of its design the comedy and tragicomedy are conspicuous, even in the final draft. In so far as the story is of Sir Austin it follows a pattern ranging from farce in the early pages to the later tragicomedy, in which an inflexible egoist comes at last to see that he has made mistakes in judgment but remains the victim of his own unimaginative attitude. It is bitter irony that the baronet's attempt to be a god to his son loses his affection entirely, that his unappreciative acceptance of women's adoration is succeeded by their denunciation of his cruelty.

There are major aspects of Richard's career which, as we have seen, are comic. His patronizing of Lucy as if she were an innocent child at the very time that he is scolding her for lack of courage, his tasting forbidden fruit as a self-appointed moralist, his self-castigation with which he gets pity from Lucy instead of the full penance he deserves, and his egoistic risking of Lucy's happiness in a duel to defend his *amour-propre* —all these are the stuff of bitter comedy. Indeed it is essentially comic that the boy who was to be guided by his father with scientific wisdom does not shape his life according to any intellectually conceived order, but instead rushes headlong, finding bliss only to desert it and careen into folly, and, like all the other Feverels, blaming fate for his ordeal, until the final overthrow, when the tragicomic muse at last waves him "for the loftier lyre."

The excellence of the novel is, however, in the psychological insight and in the subtle poetic tone, by means of which, even when the comedy is most rampant, the author never allows us to forget the spirit of romance or to doubt that Richard does have within him the capacity for tragic purification. As a lad he represents eternal boyhood, with its love of adventure, its humiliations, and its heroic loyalties. As a youth he is a knight-errant, with his passion and folly and his inherent decency. Finally, his is the tragic sorrow of a sensitive and noble mind.

Because of Meredith's indifference to tight dramatic structure Richard is sometimes a shadowy figure, whose actions are reported as having happened, with only general hints as to their motivation. But he becomes vividly real whenever we see him immediately before us and feel that we know the impressions in his mind. It is the novel's penetration of a mind rather than its surface pattern which makes it distinctive. We know what dreams Richard brings to the weir and the lyric exaltation which sustains him in a world of romance. We sense the images in his mind which inspire the pummeling of Benson, who would destroy that world. As he reads Clare's diary we know what the life is that he recalls; the diary itself is replete with images each of which can evoke companion images in Richard's mind. With his memory of his infidelity to Lucy, Richard is so vividly before us in the German forest that we experience with him both the memory and the urge to flee it. We see into the mind of the youth who has tried to make of wandering and distraction a refuge from his guilty thoughts, and we feel suddenly a hope when the discovery of the little hare brings a new group of images into his mind, images fraught with positive tenderness instead of negative remorse.

Richard has been wandering as if he were a lost soul, but the chance incident makes him a man of action, impelled by his love of his wife. When we are almost ready to believe that the reawakened love will triumph over the bitterness, Meredith tears Richard's mind apart by news of Mountfalcon's perfidy, which introduces yet a different pattern, involving both remorse and desire for action madder and more tragic than before. Finally, when fever has blotted out many images and has killed all passion to act, Richard lies before us stripped of illusion. Here Meredith, through Lady Blandish's letter, gives only the briefest statement of his hero's sense of shame and of his deepened love; for Richard is now completely tragic, and, so far as sensitive, experienced minds are concerned, his thoughts and feelings are universal.

The ornamental framework of the novel possesses a certain charm, though one would prefer a more Doric simplicity, and it does remind one that the novelist is not naïve—that he is wiser than the Wise Youth, that he sees with scientific analysis the fallacy of Sir Austin, the pretender to scientific wisdom, that he can discourse philosophically of life's passions, in short, that he draws on the disciplines of reason and common sense. But the psychological beauty is what transcends these. As we live in Richard's thoughts we feel anew that youth, adventure, love are magical qualities. We are forced relentlessly to admit that life may be a ruthless destroyer of the magic; and yet, in the paradox of tragedy, we perceive that through the chill, melancholy disillusionment about his own volatile nature and the mutability of a star-crossed fate man may still apprehend, however poignantly, a beauty which is not mutable.

Chapter Nine

Conspiracy of the Comic and Tragic Muses

In tragic life, God wot,
No villain need be! Passions spin the plot!
We are betrayed by what is false within.
(Modern Love)

If comedy and tragedy are imagined as contiguous kingdoms, then persons whom Meredith called tragic comedians dwell in the marches, an area imprecisely defined and of wide expanse. For if what is false within brings tragic disaster the falseness may still be comic.[27] The author's perspective is involved, and it expresses itself most obviously as a matter of tone.

Sir Austin, for example, is at first a merely comic character. It is his own comic fault that his wife has preferred a worthless poet to him, even as, later, it is Sir Willoughby's that Constantia and then Clara flee. But unlike Willoughby's, Sir Austin's fault leads to misfortunes that cannot be remedied—to Lucy's death and complete alienation from his son. What is left is a future of being blown about by the winds of Hell. His comic rationalizations, his self-nursings, do not anchor him, for he has lost all affinity with mankind and hence is tragic. Richard, too, is sometimes both tragic and comic, for even in his entanglement with Bella he is reminiscent of the comic chap who once went rick-burning. If he were a man of less noble personality and if no other lives were involved, the episode could be merely comic in much the way of Shibli's adventure in the hall of maidens. It is the involvement that brings tragedy; and when the author, having completed his analysis of Richard's folly, moves on to its results, the mock-epic irony is supplanted entirely by a tragic seriousness of tone.

Meredith did not succeed in making tragicomedy more profound psychologically than traditional tragedy. In achieving the intense emotional katharsis that accompanies pure tragedy, as in Richard's sorrow, the novelist excluded all other considerations to dwell upon the essential tragic emotion. In tragicomedy, on the other hand, he arrived at a katharsis of less intensity, because the intellectual analysis which tragicomedy requires prevented complete absorption in the one single tragic emotion. For loss of depth the novelist would have tragicomedy compensate by breadth of implication.

There were indeed very real artistic limitations in Meredith's depiction of falseness within. For one thing, when he examined the complex inconsistency in a mind he was often led into discursiveness. More important, he employed the tragicomic method at times in an arbitrary manner. In *Sandra Belloni,* for example, he used it for minor characters and built to minor climaxes, only to turn back to the main substance of the novel, the romantic adventure. In *Diana of the Crossways,* despite his stress on the intense pathos of Diana's suffering, he gave comic analysis of her faults and then, instead of finding a solution in tragedy, substituted the anticlimactic purging of these faults through romantic love. With certain other characters he also proceeded in a direction that should lead to tragedy, since they have serious falseness within, and yet, since his main interest was elsewhere, he did not give them their full tragic due.

In two of Meredith's pronouncedly tragicomic works—his narrative in verse *Modern Love,* 1862, (revised slightly in 1892 and 1898) and *The Tragic Comedians,* 1880—the unity fortunately did not suffer; and though in the poem there is uncertain progression, so that some stanzas might be slightly rearranged, both narratives build rapidly to the tragic ending.

The climax in *Modern Love* is the suicide of the wife and the dejection of the husband. Its poignancy is the greater because it represents a waste of lives which should instead have been rich and even ecstatically beautiful. The two were lovers once, each drawn by a quality in the other which neither has found elsewhere. As death approaches, the wife forgets the incompatibility that has wrecked their lives and knows only the sorrow of parting from the one she has deeply loved:

> "Now kiss me, dear! it may be, now!" she said.
> Lethe had passed those lips, and he knew all.

The last stanza summarizes what has gone before and designates what has already been implicit, the comic folly deep-seated in human lives:

> Thus piteously Love closed what he begat:
> The union of this ever-diverse pair!
> These two were rapid falcons in a snare,
> Condemned to do the flitting of the bat.
> Lovers beneath the singing sky of May,
> They wandered once; clear as the dew on flowers:
> But they fed not on the advancing hours:
> Their hearts held cravings for the buried day.
> Then each applied to each that fatal knife,
> Deep questioning, which probes to endless dole.
> Ah, what a dusty answer gets the soul
> When hot for certainties in this our life!—

It is the "deep questioning" which is at once comic and fatal. Each has represented to the other the soaring spirit symbolized by a falcon, but each has also asked the impossible. A falcon is a thing to be wondered at as it masters the air; one would like to capture it and have its beauty forever. But the bird ensnared is not the epitome of beauty which entranced the soul; it is discovered to be a common thing, with scarred talons and wind-blemished wings, and, more seriously, a sharp beak with which it strives to regain its freedom. In the poem the husband speaks of his having captured such a falcon. He cannot bring himself to restore its liberty; indeed he cannot feed "on the advancing hours," but lives only in bitter disillusionment about the loss of the past.

He is less easy to distinguish from the sentimentalists, such as Richard II, than from an Othello, yet his sentimentalizing has none of the simple naïveté of Richard's. In fact, he describes his own nature when he accuses women of being "destroyed by subtleties." There is something in him of Sir Austin in his seeing shrewdly general truths about mankind and yet being unable to correct his own error. There is much too of the later Wilfrid Pole, both in his fastidiousness and in his self-conscious concern for appearance.

Hamlet can speculate on revenge and Othello can acquiesce in eavesdropping, but each in so doing is largely self-forgetful, and even King Richard does not much examine his feelings until his fall. But Meredith's husband is rather more like the hero of "Locksley Hall" or, except for the madness, the hero of *Maud*. Only in his recollection do we glimpse his former happy state; within the narrative he examines and cultivates each feeling which disillusionment has inspired. He remembers that there once was happiness, and he pities his wife because she has lost it. Yet he hates her for the loss. Again, though she cannot reinspire love, he is passionately jealous because she has a lover. He enjoys the ghastly irony of her donning with him a mask before the world, and because he believes that she is not entirely acting a part, that she does still love him, he contemplates with pleasure the pain which he inflicts upon her. He may well suspect that her lover brings no comfort, for he himself is most bitter when he thinks of his own second attempt to be happy in love. He cannot adore his new mistress as he loved his wife, for he feels that he is stooping and he despises himself for the act. He flaunts his impassioned cynicism and enjoys the impression which it makes. Then, with comic inconsistency, he glamorizes his self-contempt as if he were an heroic victim destined for a sinister fate.

Othello calling his wife strumpet is not comic; one thing in his life has meant so much that its loss is intolerable. The husband in *Modern Love,* who alternately forgets himself to recall that there was a loveliness in the past which he helped destroy, and then egoistically launches into a sentimental tirade against his wife, is of a lower order. Yet we do not necessarily pity him less because we perceive his cruelty and comic inconsistency. The poet lets him speak of the beauty which the couple once found in nature and found because their minds were affined, and the pathos of its loss is intense. As they wander in the twilight listening to the swallows they do not think happily of the past—it is a buried time—but they live just enough in memory to sense that together they once knew a thrill which is forever gone:

> We had not to look back on summer joys,
> Or forward to a summer of bright dye:
> But in the largeness of the evening earth
> Our spirits grew as we went side by side.
> The hour became her husband and my bride.
> Love, that had robbed us so, thus blessed our dearth! . . .
> Love, that had robbed us of immortal things,
> This little moment mercifully gave,
> Where I have seen across the twilight wave
> The swan sail with her young beneath her wings.

But it is in the very next lines that the husband comments that women are "destroyed by subtleties." His wife has left him that he may wed the other woman, and the consequence is tragicomic torment. He calls her "this agony of flesh" and adds, "I do adore the nobleness! despise/ The act!" He is, indeed, still very much a comic creature, capable at one moment of the most exquisite sensation of beauty and in the next of the most petty, spiteful thoughts. Because he cannot see his own absurdity he cannot be cured by any experience short of tragedy. This is brought him by his wife's death. Then all his tragicomic crying at the sky subsides as the poet affixes the tragic comment "and he knew all."

The facts in Meredith's own life show the incompatibility of two remarkably subtle minds. Whether the poet felt compelled to write the poem or only recognized from his own experience that the subject matter was valid, he certainly examined sensations which were intimately connected with his own past. We must remember that he later stated that Sir Willoughby's nature was drawn from the novelist himself. But an author never merely recreates past sensations; he creates as he goes, and in any event therefore an autobiographic incident becomes a new thing each time it is summoned up. *Modern Love* is significant because, starting with a hero as sensitive and brilliant as the poet could create and thus as like his creator in poetic subtlety as it was possible to make him, Meredith indicated his ideals and then, often through the hero's own revelations, analyzed his human inconsistency. The ending is in the tone of traditional tragedy, with the author's concluding summary resembling the final comments in Shakespeare. But the substance of the poem is the psychological introspection. This substance is more inclusive than the simple pathos or tragedy which we considered in chapter seven. There are innumerable points where, because the hero *is* of a lower order, despite his sensitivity and brilliance, his words and feelings strike home and reveal how ubiquitous is the temptation for man to become false within.

In *Sandra Belloni* Meredith took time for two tragicomic progressions. The one brings into sudden prominence a minor character, Purcell Barrett, a sentimentalist explicitly identified among the "little people" with whom much of the novel is concerned. It is Barrett who speaks for the novelist himself in objecting to "the Puritan element" in literature and in approving for fiction a prose style which suggests "any mediaeval phantasy of clothing," a style which, in contrast to the "classical robe" of scientific writing, was Meredith's own. Barrett also wins our pity, for he is the son of a "flighty" mother and a nearly-insane father, and has had to submit to the whimsical tyranny of the latter. Like his now-dead mother a lover of music, he has been forbidden it by his father, and because he would not obey has been living in near poverty.

But though, as in *The Ordeal,* the parental evil is the fountain head, Meredith is concerned with Barrett's own acts. Instead of rebelling openly or bowing with patience, he has kept pent within him a rebellious feeling which has made him egoistic in a twisted way. A gentleman despite his poverty, he seeks the heart, though never actually the hand, of Cornelia Pole, having nothing to offer but a love of the arts and an idealization of womanhood. Cornelia, another little person, would accept poverty, but Purcell passively lets her become affianced to Sir Twickenham and then, with sentimental egoism, demands that she wound her fiancé's pride and bring distress to her sick father by announcing that she loves Purcell. When, too, at his father's death the disinherited Purcell, now a baronet, is offered by his uncle a fair annuity from an inheritance rightfully his own, he refuses it, not from generosity but from self-glorification; he likes his role. His major defect is an absolute refusal to face the truth. Meredith explains in his extensive exposition that even the father's insane tendency becomes for Purcell not a weakness to be pitied but one more manifestation of a malign fate. His relations with Cornelia are also an evasion. She is miserable because he treats her as an ideal of "mechanical correctness." Once he is about to expose her to herself, but this would mean examining her human faults, and so, out of kindness to himself, he refrains. Meredith calls cynicism "the younger brother of sentiment and inheritor of the family property." Purcell is at first mainly a sentimentalist, but under pressure he becomes a cynic too.

In the chapter "The Tragedy of Sentiment," which leads up to his eventual suicide, the baronet is revealed in both roles. The novelist's summary of his attitude is pertinent because it applies to other tragicomedians as well:

> The reproaching of Providence by a man of full growth, comes to some extent from his meanness, and chiefly from his pride. He remembers that the old Gods selected great heroes whom to persecute, and it is his compensation for material losses to conceive himself a distinguished mark for the Powers of air. One who wraps himself in this delusion may have great qualities; he cannot be of a very contemptible nature; and in this place we will discriminate more closely than to call him fool.

In his suppression of his feeling of injustice Barrett has become one of those who "lock up a feeding devil in their hearts," something which "little people," the author stresses, cannot safely do.

The man has thriven only while self-important, and his egoism causes him at one time to talk exaltedly about the building of soul and at another to debase himself by demanding, through cowardice and sentimental self-worship, what is really the humiliation of Cornelia. She is to risk further clandestine meetings although their talk consists mainly of Barrett's accusations that Cornelia prefers Sir Twickenham and her father to him. Yet he kisses her as a friend rather than a lover, and she is left upon the rack.

Now, upon overhearing a servant's remark which he interprets to mean that Cornelia is to be married, Purcell plans his final act. Just as he has been careful to brush his clothes and play immaculately the part of impoverished, fate-persecuted gentleman, so he dramatizes meticulously his plot for the final overthrow of fate. He is free, he reasons, because he can at any time end all. But Cornelia must be his audience, and so in a letter which contains a veiled reference to suicide, a missive carefully rewritten in an attempt to be at once casual and terrifying, he asks for yet another interview by the "fruitless tree."

That he hopes the implications will bring Cornelia and that he thinks even of asking her hand is clear from his writing a second ambiguous letter, which says in effect that he will accept the proffered annuity "for the sake of winning the highest prize humanity can bestow." Next he loads two pistols, but significantly he decides to unload one. Death, even if invited, must not be a certainty, else wherein shall fate appear. Then he lies down "with a luxurious speculation on the choice any hand might possibly make of the life-sparing or death-giving of those two weapons." In a half slumber he imagines hearing shots and seeing a woman kneel over a corpse. The next morning Karaz as flea bothers him in the form of a stupid servant girl, who recommends a fresh country egg for breakfast, and her mistress, whose sane and practical advice about tea and other "creature comforts" distracts from the tragedy he is trying hard to perform. With the thought that by a touch of her hand Cornelia can bring him back to life to let him enjoy the fire laid for his evening pleasure, he seizes a pistol, not knowing which.

That Purcell's death should result when Cornelia does not come to the tryst is only superficially a matter of chance; for he is obsessed with martyrdom, and for one who has his unstable mental heritage suicide is not too strong a form. Though possessed of a sensitive, cultivated mind, he has actually renounced life by refusing to live it freely. Preoccupation with his own image has from the beginning been an unconscious withdrawal, and the pistol shot is but the melodramatic, yet farcical conclusion for a mind that has lived upon and finally devoured itself.

The other tragicomic study in the novel is of old Pole. When playing the role of pastoral squire to the neighboring farmers and villagers, Pole seems to be a whimsical but good-natured extrovert. As a sick, lonely man trying to find amusement at the theater he is genuinely pathetic. The picture of his breakdown in health, which reduces him from an active business executive to a helpless, superannuated old man is yet more pathetic, for in the blow which suddenly strikes he experiences what all men may live to face. His loneliness has been intensified by the certainty that his children have really no deep affection for him, that in their kindness they are moved by conflicting pity and self-concern. With his sudden aging this realization too becomes more acute. There is only one person who loves him—the vulgar and impractical, but honest and generous Mrs. Chump.

What makes Pole tragicomic is that he cannot be honest in return. With all his presumed talent for business, he has lost not only most of his own money but much of Mrs. Chump's. Yet for the sake of his children, or rather to escape their reproachful thoughts, he considers marrying her. The courtship is somewhat in the Aguecheek fashion, but with tragic seriousness. To persuade the widow that he is still young and marriageable and, even more, by deceiving her to deceive himself, the old man takes long draughts from the bottle and for a little while of an evening escapes into a world of pretense, only to come back to a drink-worsened reality.

It is the dishonesty in Pole's nature that in the crisis is mastering his life. In business as elsewhere he has never been frank with anyone, and his efforts have been to gain at the expense of others or, when loss appeared certain, to evade the criticism which he deserved. It has been an image of an ideal Pole that he has with great effort paraded before the world, and it is the real Pole who pays the price. Finally the mask becomes insupportable and in the presence of his children, Mrs. Chump, and the very servants themselves Pole calls himself "an impostor! a beggar! a peculator!" It is a much more resigned, though not perfectly frank man who, extricated by Emilia's intervention, sends the widow £2000 and instead of asking her hand advises her to learn how to manage.

In Pole, Meredith was working with the consequences of rebellion against truth and the inevitability of nature, a rebellion which was to become symbolized again in Richmond Roy and also, much later, in Victor Radnor. Inasmuch as Roy is a character scarcely removed from the world of symbolic romance he cannot be examined in the same manner as Barrett or Pole. He represents a magnification of one side of Harry Richmond's nature and is seen almost entirely through Harry's eyes. That he is corrupt is illustrated in a score of ways. Often while posing as a gentleman he employs treachery and ruthlessness, and he is also at times a cheap buffoon. Yet he brings to people's lives an exhilarating air of gallant chivalry, and he dies trying to rescue the woman who has unwaveringly loved him. We cannot say that a simple tragic portrait of Roy would be less profound than what Meredith has given, but for the novelist himself the tragicomic method was the subtler.

A staunch disciplinarian of the ego, the novelist would never compromise in matters of ethics. Roy's unscrupulousness is wrong, both in its consequences for others and in its enslavement of Roy himself. It is involved, however, with a Midsummer-Night quest to turn life from an uninspired existence to a fairyland of enchantment. Consequently, though we deplore Roy's lack of ethics, we are not permitted by Meredith to reduce living to the mere following of ethical formulae. Without ethics life is not sound, but without imagination it is sterile.

For the boy Harry his father is mainly a delightful hero. True, he uses crape without proper respect for mourning and he impersonates royalty on a carriage trip. He also leaves bills unpaid and vanishes to debtors' prison. But he thrills the lad with dramatic impersonations and the hilarious stories which he spins. He is, moreover, a constant inventor of surprise. The "serio-comic" element in his nature, to use Meredith's own term, is epitomized early in the novel in the scene where, to oblige a margravine and also to enjoy a hoax, he disguises himself as a bronze statue, only to break suddenly from his pose at the unexpected sound of Harry's voice. He is indeed forever an actor. When Beltham finally calls him a "damned low vulgar comedian," who is training his son "for a swindler," Roy dramatizes his humiliation. He is a broken man, "a fallen tree"; but, Harry continues, "his inveterate fancifulness led him to add, 'And that may bridge a cataract'." He is pierced to the heart, but he feebly regains his poise and makes no further plea for sympathy. It is after this terrible scene that Harry sums up what the affair of the statue and all the other incidents have revealed: "My father was never insincere in emotion."

Roy believes that he is of royal blood though the belief implies illegitimacy. With the premise that his anonymous source of funds is the government trying to bribe him, he assumes magnificent extravagance as his social responsibility. His ideal is a tyrant's superiority to tradesmen's rules and even to those of gentlemen, as they thwart the free expansion of his soul. Ironically, he is a slave to convention, because he measures success in terms of social prestige. More seriously perhaps, he would transcend nature itself. Harry remarks that Roy did not look back, but lived in his dreams of the future. When past sixty—and at sixty he has lived a long, strenuous life—he tries to disguise from himself the coming on of age. Always subject to sudden depression, from which he would rally to cheer Harry, he now resorts to stimulants: "I am not tired; but I want my wine." There is a story that Frank Harris, who refused to accept old age, could in a second of forgetfulness become transformed into a haggard, frightened old man, only to recover self-possession and assume a cheerful youthfulness. So it is with Roy.

When Harry, even before the catastrophe, thinks of his father's life, he sees in it "elements of antique tragedy." It is such a concept of tragedy, with its stress on character, that Harry himself, like his father, would inconsistently deny—"what my incessant mental efforts were strained to expel from the idea of our human life. The individual's freedom was my tenet of faith; but pity pleaded for him that he was well-nigh irresponsible, was shamefully sinned against at his birth. . . ." Later, but still before the catastrophe, Harry is yet more penetrating: "I knew, nevertheless, that to the rest of the world he was a progressive comedy: and the knowledge made him seem more tragic still." Harry has finally to accept antique, that is, character tragedy and to pity his father within its terms, and this when most aware of Roy's—and his own—ludicrous folly.

Having maintained that Roy's life itself was a tragedy, Meredith chose not to give it an antique ending. To bring the man to either a penitent or a sordid death for his sins would have meant heavy, and to the author unconvincing, poetic justice. Though after his humiliation Roy does think for the first time of kindness to others, he is not one to recall his sins and repent them. He never again takes the initiative in extravagance, but he passively follows Harry's lead. He is, in short, not so much repentant as unhappy and resigned. He cannot live as a royal scion, and he cannot regain his youth. His death is melodramatic, yet in character. It is a dim revival of the earlier spirit that makes him decorate the house for a spectacular celebration of Harry's homecoming, and it is a typical impractical flourish in the grand manner that carelessly sets the decorations afire. Believing confusedly that his sister-in-law is within, Roy is once again the actor of gallant parts, who never dreams of caution. In the excitement of action he has always sought escape from himself, and this final act is in agreement with a lifetime habit. Though the noblest of his career, it is not one to erase his sins. There is nothing in the attempt at rescue which Roy the actor, who was nevertheless always sincere in his emotions, would not have done at any time in his life. And the character traits which lead to it are serio-comic.

In *The Tragic Comedians,* 1880, Meredith focused exclusively on tragicomedy and so delineated its characteristics that there remained only variations yet to explore. As his subtitle, "A Study in a Well-Known Story," indicated, he drew on actual incidents for touchstones. Helene von Dönniges married the man who in a duel had killed her lover, and later she attempted to narrate the episode. In a few major incidents Meredith's story follows hers, but the psychological analysis of motivation was essentially his own.[28]

In presenting his hero and heroine, both of whom are actors sincere in emotion, the novelist adopted a style in accord with their habits of mind. It has a supercharged tone, and it never slows to the natural pace of common life. The histrionic style fits protagonists who try to live in an exciting world of make-believe and consider ordinary existence a stultification.

The initial portrait of Alvan is of a great statesman, a man of action, Jewish by race but superior to racial concern, who is determined to revolutionize government to give greater independence to even its humblest citizens. Adored by women, he is still waiting to find his intellectual compeer among them. Envied by men, he is above their conventional standards. Dueling, for example, he scorns, and he can prove by his superb marksmanship that he is inspired not by fear but by contempt for unruly human passions. He is a scientist in government and in all relations with men. Physically fit and qualified, he boasts, to reach the age of eighty, he feels himself a child of destiny. He will achieve great deeds, but he has a premonition that his meteoric career will be cut off by death at forty years.

Gradually we discover that the first portrait, presented as it is by Alvan's own conversation, is inaccurate. He is eloquent, but not heroic. He takes pride in his race, but also believes himself the greater for surviving its handicap. His revolution will replace other leaders with himself, and he has never learnt what the average citizen wants; he cannot find out because he scoffs at common minds. Though he contrasts himself with the *Wilhelm Meister* concept of Hamlet as a man powerless to act, he is himself no Fortinbras. He has done a deed of serviceable intrigue for a woman, but he has unchivalrously accepted money as his reward; and though morally obligated to the woman, he ignobly refers to her—again significantly in allusion to Hamlet—as an Ophelia of fifty. Before his story is over he sacrifices his career and stakes his life to win Clothilde, yet he calls her "only a girl" and then, still wanting her, denounces her for a harlot. Contemptuous of all social conventions, he will nevertheless not carry Clothilde away when she thrusts herself upon him, but sends her home that she may be given to him conventionally at the altar. Scornful of passion and in the drawing room poised like a seraph, he falls at other times into a violent rage and bellows like a schoolboy bully. Finally, he demands satisfaction for a fancied wrong, and when Marko, not a party to the quarrel and unskilled with pistols, consents to meet him as a substitute for Clothilde's father, Alvan is unconcerned that because of his own skill the duel should be murder. It is his succumbing to the baser element in his nature that brings his death. Not the scientist but a wrathful, rebellious madman is fatally injured by the reluctant Marko. Alvan is a child of destiny doomed to die early because, in a grander manner than Purcell Barrett, he invites his own destruction.

Meredith stresses the fact that Alvan is a giant but not a hero. If he could see himself accurately and accept his limitations, he might become heroic; but he is forever trying to act a part. Even when derided by Clothilde's mother in language that recalls Beltham's to Roy, he assumes a pose of injured dignity and contempt for his accuser. Yet, actor though he is, he cannot understand Clothilde, for he never realizes that she too is an actress. The part he would play is magnificent, and through his attempt we glimpse something much more heroic than routine life. But he never really loses concern for the "philistine" world he would despise, and so he is both a robber baron or oriental tyrant and a philistine slave. It is the war between his two natures which his calm scientific pose can only for a while disguise. When it breaks into fury he is more ruthless than a barbarian.

The phrases describing him are carefully selected to define the tragicomic. At the very beginning Meredith writes, "A Faust-like legend might spring from him: he had a devil." But his devil is not without his ludicrous aspects. Of Alvan and Clothilde the author continues, ". . . the comic in their natures led by interplay to the tragic issue." The comedy is in the contrast between the pretense and the actual and even between pretenses themselves. When Alvan insists on having Clothilde bestowed upon him instead of taking her, Meredith refers by way of *Othello* to the casting away of a jewel of unknown worth, and to the villain who "refused the gift of the gods" because it was not on his own terms. He continues, "They laugh! By Orcus! how they laugh! The laughter of the gods is the lightning of death's irony over mortals. Can they have a finer subject than a giant gone fool?" Of the cause of tragedy he writes, "The two men composing it [Alvan's personality], the untamed and the candidate for citizenship, in mutual dissension pulled it down. . . . A stormy blood made wreck of a splendid intelligence." And he further defines Alvan's nature as that of "a tragic comedian: that is, a grand pretender, a self-deceiver." Particularly significant is the account of Alvan's death: "There was no interval on his passage from anguish to immobility." The man's life has for a long time been a fever. Physical suffering supplants mental torment, and there is, at the end, no peace of mind, no philosophic retrospect, no word or gesture to show deepening of understanding, nothing like Lear's "thank you, sir." A meteor has simply burnt out.

Clothilde's weakness is revealed in her contrasting feelings toward Alvan and Marko. The latter is one of Meredith's several patient young men who stand by to assist a woman in her search for independence, and to Clothilde he is unheroic. She dreams of "one who will dominate *me*." Slightly Jewish, but anti-Semitic in her prejudices, she wants not to reason about them, but to be so overwhelmed emotionally by the personality of Alvan that her irrational dislike of Jews will give way to an equally unreasoning admiration for their leader. Before meeting the great man she uses many phrases which are also his, for they both believe themselves part of a revolutionary movement and read the same articles. Not an original thinker, Clothilde is flattered to be treated as one, and she finds that Alvan carries her "more and more out of her actual into her imagined self."

A sentimentalist, she must luxuriate in her sensations, and in her egoism she is capable of exquisite cruelty. Knowing that Marko loves her, she asks him for an opinion on love, giving a hypothetical case which he cannot fail to see is her own. When Alvan ignobly demands that she rather than he write to the baroness who loves him, she assumes the childlike naïveté to write with crass candor. Like other Meredithian sentimentalists, she turns from one extreme to another, once picturing herself in a cloister; betrothal to Marko is a substitute. Of her feeling for Alvan the author editorializes, "Was it love? It was as lofty a stretch as her nature could strain to." Even in speaking truth she acts a part. It is in a self-conscious, histrionic manner that she tells Alvan that she is "three parts an actress." She wants to experience sensations and hence must act the role which should express them. When the clash occurs between her mother and Alvan, she wants to be rescued instead of planning to rescue herself. Even in her thoughts she evades coming to grips with problems. Meredith sometimes prints dots to show her mind starting on a line of thought only to wander off in vagueness because further thinking would be unpleasant. It is in such instances here and in the later works that one wishes the novelist had dared to replace the dots with the images which succeeded each other as the mind sought refuge in semiconsciousness.

Clothilde is powerless when Alvan makes of her a demand as unreasonable as Purcell Barrett's of Cornelia—that, betrothed to another, she send him attestation of her love. The request destroys her magnificent illusion of being dominated and freed from making decisions. She can only once again act a part, hoping that he will understand. Her own vanity has been wounded, and in her anguish she cries out against the vanity of her lover. Yet, humiliated and angry though she is, she must preserve her illusion that Alvan is an heroic person. She must blame others, not him, for the death of Marko, which she expects to result from the duel. Characteristically, though she cannot think upon the tragic nature of the duel, she sees in anticipation all the details of the announcement of Marko's death. When told instead that Alvan is wounded, she laughs as one not able to come back from the imagined to the actual: "It was the laugh of the tragic comedian." For his death she blames her parents; she "accepted them as proper substitutes for her conscience." Reduced by misery to "nothingness," she weds Marko in the hope of doing some good, but she loves Alvan still. She is the passive cause of her own misfortune in that she cannot act simply and honestly when independence of action is needed. She suffers the more because, with her habit of vacillation, she cannot extricate herself. Like Alvan, she is not purified at the end. She is only somewhat wiser; and in words reminiscent of those which he used in *Rhoda Fleming* and *Sandra Belloni* about the "little people," the novelist remarks that "we are in her debt for some instruction."

Between *The Tragic Comedians* and Meredith's last three completed novels comes *Diana of the Crossways.* In chapter seven we noticed aspects of Diana's history which were comic and also the nervous collapse to which her own foolish actions contributed. There are several scenes in the novel which reveal the heroine denying her real nature in a desperate effort to be a man among men. These are both comic in appearance and tragic in implication. The significant difference between Diana, however, and Clothilde and the other tragicomedians of the present chapter is that there is very fine substance within her. An acute shock, which includes some self-condemnation and intense grief, shatters illusions, and then a long, slow —and artistically anticlimactic—process of rebuilding under the aegis of romance brings out her best. But even in the midst of her folly Meredith stresses her capacity for love and self-forgetful friendship. She is only for a while a "self-deceiver." In portraying her the novelist was simply employing a method of analysis which he was finding more and more fruitful. He believed that he could best present the serious but curable confusion in Diana's mind by showing its comic incongruity with her inherent impulse toward sanity.

On the other hand, Meredith's last three major tragicomedians—Lord Ormont, Fleetwood, and Victor Radnor—join with Alvan to make an impressive quartet of self-deceivers. The four represent the statesman, the soldier, the man of rank and inherited wealth, and the business man who is a social parvenu. They are all deluded as to their own natures and their places in the universal scheme of things, and all except Alvan are depicted in contrast to their romantic, clear-eyed opposites—Aminta, Carinthia, and Victor's daughter, Nesta. *One of Our Conquerors* is too complex for brief discussion, but Ormont and Fleetwood are only variations of a pattern. The Ormont idolized by the schoolboy Weyburn is the magnificent working soldier; actually, as we come to learn, he has used strong-arm, autocratic methods in India. The Ormont whom Weyburn's school-girl beloved marries is Weyburn's idol, who is assumed to be possessed of all the lad's own chivalry toward girls; actually he is one who in relations with women has enjoyed possession without responsibility. Rebuked by Government, he becomes a sulking Coriolanus—Meredith's own identification of him; and though now married, he expresses his scorn of society by refusing to take Aminta into it or to install her in his ancestral home. The motivation is not altogether convincing, but the author wishes to present Ormont devoid of occupation and reduced to playing a game of "pull," in which he, the self-styled master of women, is really their comic victim.

As a Coriolanus he substitutes pen for sword and tries to attack Government in his memoirs, but even he comes to realize that his sentimental diatribes are self-exposures. In his war with society he is no match for women. His Amazonian sister, opposed to recognition of Aminta, and Aminta's vulgar aunt, determined upon it, create circumstances for Ormont which are a constant embarrassment. Still cherishing a fondness for pretty faces, which in no way reduces his contempt for women, Ormont is actually Aminta's victim, even as a miser is the slave of his hoard. He once calls her a jewel, and, asked by her what jewels are for, replies, "To excite cupidity." He eventually sums up his predicament with the remark that he is having to fight with "bodkins."

Like Alvan, Ormont is a comic giant who has thrown away his career among men and, because he is really ignorant of women, finds himself helpless among them. It is his refusal to recognize himself as a common citizen and his "massive selfishness and icy inaccessibility to emotion" as a husband that prevent his finding romance. He is still foolishly defensive, even when in an irate reversal of tactics he determines to force Aminta into society. Only when this act of supreme egoism makes her leave him does he discover what a jewel he has cast away.

Meredith arbitrarily allots to Ormont a steady sobering during the years before the narration picks up his story again. Despite his former selfishness Aminta, we are told, comes to respect him as a "true noble" man, and it is a wiser and gentler Ormont who sends his grand-nephew to Weyburn's and Aminta's school. The katharsis of his cynical egoism is, however, rather asserted than proved. It seems dictated by the author's wish to justify Aminta's liaison with Weyburn and to avoid a bitter note in the novel's romantic conclusion. At the end of the main action Ormont is not a philosophical person, but an egoist who has been stripped of self-respect and left to writhe in tragicomic despair.

The Earl of Fleetwood, in *The Amazing Marriage,* is constructed mainly from characteristics already to be found in other Meredithian comic and tragicomic characters. Like Sir Willoughby, he is a man of wealth, indeed fabulous wealth, who has an air of elegance, a highly refined sensitivity, and a "mantle" suggesting greatness. But even more than the baronet he lacks occupation. From time to time he is revealed to have latent virtues which if exercised would lead him to an exciting, courageous life. But he has had no discipline, and having turned inward in his thoughts, he has become corrupt. He would like to think himself a master over others, and he welcomes parasites whom he can supply with money and encourage to gamble, that he may degrade them to his own level and relieve his intense boredom. His satanic tinge, from which Willoughby is free, is presumably traceable, as was Barrett's, to parental insanity; like Barrett, he cultivates melancholy. As unprincipled as Algernon Blancove, he swings, like him, from extreme to extreme, sometimes performing a deed of generosity or living a simple, elemental life as a change from cruelty and dissipation. And like Barrett, Algy, and Edward Blancove, he is very much a creature of his senations. He will not look upon nature frankly, but must color it with sentimental cynicism, glorifying himself when he turns to natural scenery in pseudo-romantic retreat from the contemptible "Ixionides" for whose corruption he has been responsible. Though he comes to find novelty in Carinthia's unsophisticated freshness, he wonders whether she can "take polish a little." With no clear concept of ideal womanhood, he is yet contemptuous of anything less. Because he can do nothing positive to make life an adventure, his sensations are never pleasant for more than brief moments, and he is forever trying to escape to new ones. And like all Meredith's other egoists, he would avoid responsibility for his actions.

It is his ruthlessness toward others, especially women, and his evasions of responsibility that make up much of Fleetwood's history. Characteristically, he once remarks that one's deeds never die, and yet he acts as if their ghosts could be laid. Meredith calls him an "oriental voluptuary," who "coveted beauty in women hungrily, and seemed to be born hostile to them." In self-excuse he invariably blames women—first Henrietta and then Carinthia—for his disillusionment. He wants Henrietta but resents his passion: "He took love unmanfully; the passion struck at his weakness; in wrath at the humiliation, if only to revenge himself for that, he could be fiendish; he knew it, and loathed the desired fair creature who caused and exposed to him these cracks in his nature, whence there came a brimstone stench of the infernal pits." Married to Carinthia, he is once more bitter: "A sour relish of the irony in his present position sharpened him to devilish enjoyment of it, as the finest form of loathing. . . . He had cried for Romance—here it was!" To try to forget Henrietta he must believe her shallow, but like a true voluptuary, he cannot really forget her and so has to substitute revenge for possession. When his sins accumulate he seeks a cowardly alternative to honest self-analysis: "He craved a scourging that he might not be cursing himself."

Fleetwood naturally fails in each crisis. When he can no longer blame circumstance and thus exonerate himself, he turns for protection to religion: "Religion," he is assured, "has a nourishing breast: Philosophy is breastless. Religion condones offenses: Philosophy has no forgiveness, is an untenanted confessional." This doctrine, taught him by his clerical friend, Lord Feltre, comes to be more and more inviting. He does meditate doing penance outside the church "in the manly fashion," to quote Meredith's commentary on his thoughts; and after a base trick on Henrietta and her husband he actually writes her a confession. But he tears up the letter and thinks of the monastery as his source of forgiveness: "It proved how men may by power of grip squeeze raptures out of pain." One recalls Edward Blancove's sentimental anticipation of the luxury of Dahlia's forgiveness. When Fleetwood avoids confessing to Carinthia, Meredith writes that, had he confessed, "she would have held hot iron to the rabid wound [an allusion to her courage and Fleetwood's cowardice when a child was bitten by a mad dog and Carinthia prescribed hot iron] and come to a love of the rescued sufferer." Fleetwood's escape into a monastery, after one final magnificently worldly fête and a final act of sensual hypocrisy, is plausible for a person of his violent and unstable temperament. But it is rather more a symbol of the tragicomedian's inability to face reality. Like all the others—except the reformed Ormont—Fleetwood is incapable of a spiritual katharsis which would leave him "calm of mind, all passion spent."

In narrating the lives of all his tragicomic characters Meredith often adopts a poetic tone. But it is not in the grand manner appropriate to a great, though evil person, nor has it the simple lyric beauty that expresses elemental sorrow. Always there is a feverish spirit in the lines to remind us that the protagonists are ill of a disease which they cannot cure because they deny its existence. The role of the author is to study minutely the symptoms, to show what the remedy should have been, and, while providing instruction through the study of characters who are either "little" persons or at most not of the stature of great heroes, to suggest to the reader a kinship that may well inspire pity and fear.

Chapter Ten

Darkness Within

In tragic hints here see what evermore
Moves dark as yonder midnight ocean's force,
Thundering like ramping hosts of warrior horse,
To throw that faint thin line upon the shore!
(Modern Love)

BOTH the title of *One of Our Conquerors,* 189[1], and the name of its tragicomic hero, Victor Radnor, are, as one should expect, ironic. Yet the irony is not patent, for Victor is neither a barbarian, like Maupassant's Bel Ami, nor a usurper who in the midst of success is cast off by his social victims. He is, instead, a courageous, sensitive, and generally conscientious man, well regarded by many sensible people; and if we did not learn his inner history, we should find him only a kindly person, who would like to compensate for a mistake made early in his career, and who is unfortunate in that he cannot manage to give up his strenuous duties as a financial and social leader to enjoy the simple, restful life for which he longs. He is, indeed, in most ways—one might hazard the suggestion in all ways—essentially like his fellow mortals, his differences being only in degree. These differences are not sufficient to make him a spectacular tragic hero, nor even to spare him the buffetings of the comic imps. They are just enough to identify for the reader certain major but normally very much disguised impulses which bring human malaise and sometimes wretchedness.

There are several defects in *One of Our Conquerors,* and at the first reading one may be tempted to agree with Richard Le Gallienne that it is in some ways "a weariness of the flesh." Meredith's fatigue during composition may be in part accountable; perhaps more responsible was a desire to push yet further an intricate method of character presentation, for though as far back as *The Ordeal* and *Modern Love* he had psychologically explored his characters, he was still experimenting with the technique. There are gaucheries in the book which rereading does not dispel—the lifeless narrative of Colney Durance; the ambiguous references to the unmarried Judith as Mrs. Marsett; the refusal to admit that the senescent Mrs. Burman, and not Nataly, is Victor's legal wife until pages after the reader has had to infer it; and a style which at times is neither subtle nor brilliant, but merely prosaically involved. But with all these and other infelicities the novel is even more than most a work that should be read at least twice. The reason is inherent in what Meredith was trying to do in this his most obtuse and yet in some respects his most profound novel.

When the story opens, the hero is in middle age, with a marriageable daughter. The mistake which he made, his unwise marriage for money, occurred in the distant past, before he fell in love with Mrs. Burman's young companion Nataly and the lovers went off to a new home as man and wife. Victor recognizes the folly of his marriage, but as his wife still refuses a divorce, he tries to believe that he has abundantly atoned. His actions, however, reveal that the mistake sprang from his own nature and that he has actually made it worse by his refusal to pay in humility and honest repentance for what he has done. Why did Victor as a young man commit folly that has shadowed his career and made him at best uneasy, at worst wretched? The novelist answers the question not in the traditional manner by tracing his hero's life before the marriage, but by examining it now. The man is the victim most certainly of that one act, but his fundamental weakness of character has not been altered by it. As he is now, so was he years before; therefore the marriage itself and all other early events in his life become understandable in the light of his thoughts and actions since.

The psychological method which Meredith used has two advantages. In the first place, it shows with concrete objectivity that the outward pattern of Victor's life, though subject to ebb and flow, with what may seem to be striking differences when measured in beach markings, is really shaped by forces underneath which in half a lifetime under the intense beating of storms and the falling of cliffs has remained in its essential nature unchanged. In the second place, while giving a glimpse of the long anxious years in between, it permits us to see that psychologically what happened twenty or more years ago is a present incident. Time as such becomes meaningless; indeed it is a wild illusion. As we enter Victor's mind we live not in a temporal realm, but in a human consciousness, a consciousness which itself tries to believe that time is real in that the present replaces the past, but is forced again and again to the sensation that the past is forever present.

The novel opens with an incident casual enough in appearance, and not until much later do we perceive that it is Victor's life in miniature. He slips while crossing London Bridge, and though grateful for a laboring man's help in regaining his feet, he is disturbed by his rescuer's careless soiling of his white waistcoat, premature apparel for a gusty first day of April. The reply to his thoughtless complaint is a yet more severe jolt: "And none of your dam punctilio." Suddenly Victor has a feeling that he is about to get hold of his "idea," but he loses it again. He once more assumes a determined manner, yet hesitates to cross a busy thoroughfare, for "once down, or once out of the rutted line, you are food for lion and jackal." When joined by a friend, however, he at once crosses, "dismissing nervousness as a vapour." A few minutes later he drinks heavily—of an expensive wine, which like the waistcoat is appropriate to a successful man who enjoys being first in all things—and is ready for his work as a financier.

Shades of old Pole, Richmond Roy, and lesser characters are conjured up by the incident, and yet Victor is no mere composite. The dictum of a physician (quoted in a letter by Meredith October 15, 1906) that in the initial episode Victor shows symptoms of "incipient lesion of brain" is pertinent not as a label of a pathological condition, for the man is not abnormal, but as an indication of the inclusiveness of the psychological portrait. Victor's actions are bound inescapably to his semiconscious apprehensions and his physical sensations, and these are always tinged with anxiety. He sometimes attempts to dissipate them by an arbitrary assertion of will, often fortified by wine, friendship, or activity. But the mental effort brings no real escape, because he is not honest with himself. He would rise above unpleasant feelings, mental and physical, and yet he would also drown unpleasant thoughts by submerging himself in sensation. The one thought which he above all cannot face is the "idea." It is this which is his obsession till the end, and he never brings himself to see it, because whenever he draws near, it becomes too terrifying.

What is this idea? To reduce hundreds of pages to a brief summary is to lose many of the nuances that go to make it up, for it is a nebulous thing, and Meredith himself prefers to define it by showing its ubiquitous importance among civilized men and the varied manifestations of its power. It is in a general way the answer to the old question of the individual's identity. Victor obviously tries to reduce the question to too narrow terms, and perhaps for that very reason its possible answer becomes the more frightening to him. He must build up an image of himself in relation to other people which has no taint of guilt and none of failure, and yet he finds that this is not his true identity. The certainty that it is not determines him only to continue modifying the illusion to evade seeing the reality.

Victor admits that his marriage with a much older and "crazy" woman was for money, and he even thinks of asking her forgiveness for his desertion; but the thought brings with it an image of the scene that would be involved, and "a sight of that extremity fetched prickles to his forehead." Indeed forgiveness would not actually contribute to his atonement; the request for it would at best serve to placate the irate woman, who is threatening social exposure. As to the money, he admits that it gave him a start toward the success which he craved, but he stresses the fact that he left his wife as rich as he found her. Moreover, he argues to himself, he gave in return his youth, and the bargain, though not a happy one for Mrs. Burman, was unfair to him.

In one of his determinedly optimistic moods Victor pictures himself as "the pick of his country for vigour, gallantry, trustiness, high-mindedness." He tries to live up to the portrait, and a year later—the main action takes about one year—he still reassures himself that he has a good conscience. He patronizes the arts and intends to give cultural gifts to the nation. He also entertains lavishly and is always bountiful in his generosity. His wife has prevented his marrying Nataly, and whenever his social success has made him prominent in a community, news of the liaison has caused a dropping away of casual acquaintances; but he has compensated for Nataly's embarrassment by showering upon her magnificent surprises, including a new, expensive country house, and he has arranged for her to assume with him once more a splendid social role. Victor wants to be liked. Since he plays the flute, he imagines Nesta's marrying a flute player from love of her father. There should be no question of Nataly's love, for he is a successful, cultivated man, whom she can respect, and he anticipates her wishes before they are spoken. He can number among his many friends even the pessimist and satirist, for Victor is willing, indeed eager, to defend his optimism against attack.

But there are symptoms which reveal that his positive manner disguises a serious insecurity. Even though he continues to speculate, he is left restless rather than exhilarated by his financial gambles: ". . . gold-mines are lodgings," he remarks, "not homes." Instead of enjoying friendship he needs it as a drug, and with it flattery such as his admiring client, Lady Grace, provides; his mild adventure in infidelity with her gives him momentarily the illusion that with her instead of Nataly beside him "it was a conquered world." But as with wine, the effect is not lasting. He rejoices in the power of Wagner, so obviously suggestive of his own wish to conquer, but as oppression grows upon him he retreats to his earlier love of the Italian composers. The liaison itself imposes a paradox upon him. He has defied conventions, yet as his remark on crossing the street reveals, he senses that he is "out of the rutted line" and so, if "once down," is "food for lion and jackal." Most oppressive of all is the dim awareness of what he cannot put consciously, his enslavement to his ambition: "Victor had yet to learn, that the man with a material object in aim, is the man of his object; and the nearer to his mark, often the farther is he from a sober self; he is more the arrow of his bow than bow to his arrow." He finds ownership and desire for social prestige making him act contrary to his taste and inclinations, yet he cannot turn or stop, but must plunge on. In Nataly's words, "he seems a man pushed by Destiny . . . his nature shrinks from the thing it calls up. He dreads the exposure he courts—or has to combat with all his powers."

Though Meredith does not use a stream-of-consciousness technique, he sketches the pattern of Victor's thoughts and their accompanying sensations. As painful as the prospect of asking forgiveness is that of explaining Nesta's illegitimacy to a prospective bridegroom—it "gripped at his vitals a minute." Characteristically, he pictures a fine settlement as compensating, yet he feels contempt for any man who would marry for it. Thought of his early life with Mrs. Burman brings physical revulsion, but when he excuses his desertion of her he is "dissatisfied with [the] verdict." Meredith goes so far as to let him once sense a plucking at his elbow that causes him to turn away from a shop where he would probably otherwise have met her. The depression which he feels when he looks back on his career expresses itself as a physical sensation: "things pleasant enough in the passage of them were barren, if not prickly, in the retrospect." In the retributive scene, when he and Nataly do go to Mrs. Burman, a veritable Miss Havisham, he is almost entirely a creature of sensation. The scent of Maréchale takes him back to unpleasant memories, and when commanded to pray, he sees his prayer "dancing across the furniture; a diminutive thin black figure. . . ." A cupid swinging on a wrongly-set clock becomes a symbol of "Time gone crazy." These are not sensations to be exorcised, because they spring hydra-fashion from his primary guilt.

In the early pages of the novel Victor is still determined to mark out for himself a line which will give order to his future life and yet free him from his past. He is thus an optimist, who will later join the pessimist Durance and the neutral Dudley Sowerby to make what Meredith calls a comic trio, comic because lacking in depth of conviction in the positions they maintain. He must believe that Nataly shares his happy confidence; yet his dream of contentment is at war with his restless egoism, and the result is confusion. He can think of a simple rural home with poultry and cows, "and a certain influence," he adds, which "one has in the country socially." His new mansion at Lakelands will be his "Sabine Farm" (Horace, according to *Beauchamp's Career,* is "the Tory's mentor"); and, with the laborer's words still lingering in his memory, he protests that he wants "a home—not empty punctilio." Yet he already sees in his mind the magnificent entertainments it will accommodate. After he has lost the need of Lady Grace he can perceive "the Goddess Nature there is in a chastened nature," though he toys with the thought of a bit more philandering with the woman. Later he wonders, "Are we, in fact, harmonious with the Great Mother when we yield to the pressure of our natures for indulgence?" Again, he can, like Beauchamp, stress the necessity of a "dispersion of wealth" and of "decent poverty." But he is not yet really chastened by nature and he is now planning a yacht trip. His tragicomic personality is defined in the author's description of his type early in the story. "The histrionic self-deceiver," says Meredith, deceives us into believing with him, "that we may be armed as he is for enjoying the coveted reality through the partial simulation of possessing it." As a self-deceiver Victor must win from others not mere toleration, but the support which they are sometimes glad to offer in order to deceive themselves. Without followers to lead he is helpless to act, and without action his optimism evaporates. Characteristically, he prefers action to analysis in fiction.

In the midst of Victor's mental wanderings the "idea," or later the "lost Idea," becomes the touchstone by which his aberration from nature is to be judged. It is like a shadow. He senses its presence as if it were physically just behind him: "since the day of the fall (never, save in merest glimpses, before that day), he had taken to look behind him, as though an eye had been knocked in the back of his head." Whenever he feels especially depressed because he is slave to his object, he comes close to the idea. Since the fall his mind has been "shadowed by doubts of his infallible instinct for success." He tries to transform his apprehended idea into a positive help: "Somewhere he had an idea, that would lift and cleanse all degradations." But it is then that the barren, prickly sensation proves him false. He associates the idea with nature's chastening and believes he will "grasp it soon." He thinks vaguely of an idea which he "once had and never quite got hold of again," and he is so obsessed that he speaks of it to Nataly; with an allusion to the "artistocracy of self-denying discipline" she strikes a "Lucifer in his darkness." He half envies caged beasts for being less annoying than the idle rich, especially the dying Mrs. Burman, whose existence they call to mind, and the comparison suggests his idea. It comes to share even his nonwaking hours: "His lost Idea drew close to him in sleep." It becomes a positive, cheerful vision when he tries to formulate it as a picture of things to come in England, with Victor leading the way to national success and cultural prosperity for all classes, a prosperity somehow untouched by materialism; but the vision is only an illusive disguise of the Idea's gloomy reality, which returns formlessly to haunt him. He now believes that he did actually see it and has merely lost it: "On London Bridge he had *seen* it. . . . That was after a fall. There had been a fall also of the scheme of Lakelands . . . there had certainly been a moral fall, fully to the level of the physical."

As Victor's mad course runs out its relentless pattern the sense of guilt becomes more and more attached to the idea, hard though he tries to deny it. When he looks back on the year at Lakelands he at first sums it up as "notwithstanding uninterrupted successes . . . a blank." But he at once realizes that it is much worse; a "black agent" demands payment. Having now gone through the scene with Mrs. Burman, he begins to feel his guilt with respect to Nataly. Yet he cannot treat her as a true partner by consulting her wishes, and he is responsible for her death when he once more courts public exposure by campaigning for Parliament. Like a frenzied giant, he wants to be married to her now that Mrs. Burman's death has succeeded hers by a few hours. He has a "confession for his Nataly . . . an Idea"; and as she can never hear it, he pleads for Dudley to listen "without any punctilio." His conduct is still a grotesque irony, not a pure, simple expression of sorrow. He is beaten and stunned, and his refusal afterward to see Nesta shows that he is ashamed. He is a much better man than before, but the purification is not yet absolute. In his grief he forgets appearances, and yet it is of himself that he is thinking as he wants the dead Nataly and then Dudley to understand; and his refusal to see Nesta reminds us of his lifetime habit of shrinking from unpleasant scenes.

Shortly before his death he does express a wish to have the girl with him. Thus the muse of Tragedy at last has compassion upon him, and only then does the muse of Comedy, a stern realist, let go her hold. It is she who has revealed to us the inconsistency, the ludicrous mental gyrations—the falseness within. And if at the end we are sure that we have seen the Idea better than Victor himself, that we know what kind of man he is and can fit him into the eternal scheme, we may, to our surprise, find ourselves glimpsing the skirts of a sister idea, from which we may shrink as intensely as Victor from his; for in Meredith's fiction the implication is always unrelentingly *de te fabula.*

Nataly seldom thinks in terms of anything so definite even as Victor's nebulous idea. Until chapter twenty-five she is rarely more than an unhappy passenger in her partner's boat, acquiescing in all his plans and keeping counsel with herself. But in her suppression of desire she becomes the creature of irreconcilable impulses. She must believe in Victor, and to do so she must blame circumstance; but she must also believe in certain principles, and in doing so she cannot escape seeing Victor's faults. Finally, without formulating an idea about it, she is wretchedly aware of something wrong with herself for which neither Victor nor circumstance in general can be blamed.

Nataly is perhaps the most striking example in Meredith's works of the paradox involved in the subjection of women. As a person who has violated a major convention she is a victim of collective woman's rigid conventionality, yet she is by nature ultraconventional. It is of just such women as herself that collective woman is composed. She is attractive and she sings well, but unlike the later Aminta, she has neither the talent nor spirit to become independent. Consequently she is deeply embarrassed by whatever makes her conspicuous. Singing at Victor's insistence distresses her, and even her ampleness of figure makes her painfully self-conscious. She is "designed by nature" for marriage, and she must both hate the institution which brands her as different from other mothers and at the same time long for its benefits for herself. Unlike Victor, she does not want to prove her superiority to convention: "Eminently servile is the tolerated lawbreaker: none so conservative." Partly because she dreads to tell her, Nataly would protect Nesta from the facts about her illegitimacy. She goes further, keeping from her any newspapers which report marital irregularities; she is sure that a bridegroom would expect innocence, and that the best safeguard of innocence is ignorance. Like Victor, she hopes for a good marriage, but when she thinks of Dudley, an affable, unobjectionable young man, she cannot wish to trap him by concealing the truth.

It is this type of conflict between nature—her natural love for Nesta—and her artificial standards that makes Nataly comically tragic. She sees an awkwardness of circumstance as if it were a defect in the girl herself, for she cannot separate the misfortunes of the daughter from the sins of the mother. To minimize the blemish would be to exculpate herself; to exaggerate it, as she does, in self-castigation is to commit a sin against the girl. Nataly's fate is so bound with the lives of others that she cannot extricate herself from the entanglement. To condemn herself is to condemn Victor; to excuse him is to be too lenient on herself. She ought to feel compassion for Judith, yet her conscience will not permit her to let Nesta love a woman who has committed Nataly's own sin; and if she let herself linger on the subject, she would have to wish that Nesta condemn her own mother. She owes a loyalty to Mrs. Burman and at first, in pity, prays for her, but perceiving the hypocrisy, she ceases. She cannot frankly pray for the woman's death, and yet her longing to be married presupposes that event.

The initial sin is, of course, not what Nataly feels it to be, except as disloyalty to Mrs. Burman is concerned. In the eyes of an author who was to send Aminta as companion to Weyburn conventions must yield to a higher law. Nataly is false within not because of her unconventionality, but because of her moral irresponsibility. When wooed by Victor she took the easiest path by letting him make decisions. Now she is as enslaved as he is, and having done without self-discipline, she is unable to assume it. Her mental sensations are as prickly as Victor's; but like him, she finds even half-articulated thoughts still more frightening, and she seeks escape by letting them fade away into formlessness. It is their ghosts which come back to haunt her. Meredith sums up the life she has had with Victor, a life constantly harassed by the fear of new experience: "she had no longer root of her own; away she sailed, through beautiful scenery, with occasionally a crashing fall, a turmoil, emergence from a vortex, and once more the sunny whirling surface." When she once tries to judge her conduct, she finds the strain too great; her judgment, Meredith comments, "whirled, swam to a giddiness and subsided." When Victor again courts exposure by building Lakelands, panic seizes her; yet she dares not think for herself and must seek refuge in reliance on his judgment. "In fine," says the author, "when the sensations are spirited up to drown the mind, we become drift-matter of tides, metal to magnets. And if we are women, . . . credulity—the continued trust in the man—is the alternative of despair."

Once Nataly insists that she does not "feel the guilt"; but she is glad for Colney Durance's scolding, since she can find comfort in believing that she does not quite deserve it. In addition to the feeling that somehow she has done wrong there is the very real terror that comes when she lets herself sense her perilous dependence on Victor. It is not that she expects him to abandon her. It is rather her increasing realization that, having made him into a god, she has no other refuge. When she thinks, for example, of his generous nature, she sees it "doomed to show signs of dross ultimately." She justifies his desertion of Mrs. Burman by insisting to herself that he could not help having a physical aversion to her, but she has increasing difficulty in thinking of Victor himself as a paragon of attractiveness. It is not that he is really inferior to Nataly, but that, having been reared to take a dependent role in life, she expects all from outside, nothing but obedience from herself. Of her false view of reality Meredith writes, "Nataly's intellect and her reverence clashed. They clash to the end of time if we persist in regarding the Spirit of Life as a remote Externe, who plays the human figures, to bring about this or that issue, instead of being beside us, within us, our breath, if we will. . . . ."

In chapter twenty-five, entitled "Nataly in Action," she begins to free herself somewhat, though from motives which she would never admit. For her it is a triumph to tell Dudley of Nesta's illegitimacy; but she has acted upon the discovery that Dartrey's wife is dead and that he may now become the husband she wants for her daughter if Dudley withdraws his suit. After the exertion, which under the circumstances is not a noble confession leading toward atonement, she sinks back again, though not quite to her former helplessness. Her subsequent bolts toward freedom are the consequence of her gradual disillusionment about Victor and her perception that she can endure it. Having in reverie imagined herself kissed by Dartrey-Victor—an incident vaguely remininiscent of *Die Wahlverwandtschaften*—she tells Dartrey that she loves him, at once adding the wish that he were her "brother or son." With Dartrey as a new god, though subject to her Platonic reservations, she is able to pronounce the damning opinion on

Victor that he seems "pushed by Destiny," in short, no longer a god or even a man on whom to lean. Now, as she gets a slight feeling of independence, she more than ever wishes for purification, and that means punishment for her sin. In her naïve, convention-ridden mind, however, the punishment again drags in her daughter. Nesta's contamination in the form of her friendship for Judith is to Nataly "divine": "I never felt my sin until this blow came!" In condemning Judith to herself she imagines that she is condemning herself before the world.

Unfortunately Nataly is no Clara Middleton, nor are the circumstances which she has accepted the kind that even a strong will could surmount. She is wedded to Victor by ties which she cannot break, indeed has no moral right to break. He has in his blind way tried to show her kindness, and she is really much at fault that he has never treated her as an equal; she has for years refused to be so treated. There are consequently for Nataly only brief sorties outside the castle walls, just enough to reveal the freedom she has missed. When Victor persists in the most grandiose and perilous of all his ambitions by campaigning for Parliament, Nataly is doomed. She has sometimes been glad that her weak heart promises her relief in death if her guilt-inspired anguish becomes too heavy to bear, and the new threat of exposure is the needed shock. Though she hoped to expiate by humbling herself before Mrs. Burman, she has not felt charitable toward her now that the ordeal is over; and there is no evidence that any real spiritual triumph precedes her death. She merely succumbs to the strain. It is with deep compassion that Meredith brings her tragedy to a close, and yet in an equally compassionate study he let the hero in *Modern Love* speak firmly for him in words that fit Nataly and all of her type:

> Their sense is with their senses all mixed in,
> Destroyed by subtleties these women are!
> More brain, O Lord, more brain!

In contrast to her parents, Nesta typifies a romantic view of life. Meredith does not account for her simple wisdom. She has been reared in a conventional home, with her mother attempting to keep her in ignorance of the world's evils. Yet she is much more tolerant than Judith, who needs the tolerance of others. Though he once approved of trial marriages, Meredith recognized the importance of conventions. Nesta has no wish to revolt against them, and indeed she helps to get Judith wedded; but like Meredith, she looks first at human nature and then at the conventions as the social expression of man's striving toward an ideal of orderly freedom. Of course, she never explains her thoughts and she is not, after all, a philosopher; but she exemplifies by her actions the views of a novelist who was. When she and Dartrey look straight into each other's eyes, Meredith states that they are "past plighting, they are the wedded one." Nataly and Victor, though bound by strange ties, imagine themselves lacking the one bond which would unite them; yet we know that marriage would have achieved no miracles, that it would have left them as unhappily mated as before. For Dartrey and Nesta the marriage ceremony is not irrelevant simply because the two are in spirit already the wedded one.

The portrait of Nesta is developed very much in terms of her sensations. Standing in the Mausoleum at Dreux she feels herself in a "forest-well of mediaeval imaginativeness," and the sound of the unctuous platitudes of the Reverend Septimus Barmby blends with the scene; but when, soon afterward, he proposes marriage, the sense of his words shatters her "mediaeval forest-palace of illuminated glass." The proposal is not a mere impertinence; the image of marital union with so unattractive a man is a wound to her sensibility, and the association in her mind causes the earlier enchantment to vanish.

It is natural for Nesta to cherish a chivalric dream of a Siegfried lover, and when she learns that the hot-tempered

Dartrey has been involved in a street fray defending an "Army" enthusiast, she suffers to a lesser degree what Rose Jocelyn endured when pronouncing "snip." But like Rose, she is sensible, and she comes to love Dartrey with no illusions and with no emotional reservations. Indeed it is generally in this manner that she faces experiences. Consequently she lives each moment intensely, with her whole being absorbed in it. For the same reason she is free of the emotional confusion which destroys Nataly and Victor. She neither drifts nor rationalizes; she has no lost idea.

The surface of Nesta's life is by no means unruffled; she is much too sensitive to miss trouble and suffering. But the forces beneath the surface are not engaged in a constant clashing. With Victor and Nataly we cannot look down through turbulent seas and are forced for our knowledge of their depths to study most carefully the "faint thin line upon the shore." With Nesta we have still the faint line, but its form is more predictable, because we see not only it but the limpid depths from which its motion comes.

In stressing in *One of Our Conquerors* the role of sensation and of the semiconscious Meredith was continuing the exploration of the mind which had characterized *Modern Love* and *The Ordeal* at the outset of his career. Yet, as in those works, he did not make of life a mere complex of sensations and subconscious impulses. Reason must prevail. What he was attempting was to distinguish reason as a power of choice from that Duessa-like phantom of reason which, in seeking to placate the senses, leaves man their slave. Comedy, romance, and tragedy were all pertinent to his task. Most illuminating of all perspectives for Meredith was one which permitted the light of comedy to penetrate to the heart of tragedy and to show how it differed from the heart of romance. In this way he could best state what he wanted to express through his art —which, in the most complete sense of the term, was always *Nosce teipsum.*

Notes

1. "Humour in its intense strain has a seat somewhere about the mouth of tragedy, giving it the enigmatical faint wry pull at a corner visible at times upon the dreadful mask." (*Celt and Saxon,* chapter six) The most thorough discussion of Meredith's comedy is by Joseph Warren Beach, *The Comic Spirit of George Meredith: An Interpretation.* For Meredith's thought as it is expressed in his poetry, cf. especially George M. Trevelyan, *The Poetry and Philosophy of George Meredith.* The most stimulating criticism of Meredith as a novelist is by Joseph B. Priestley, *George Meredith.*
2. For example, in chapter eleven of *Lord Ormont and His Aminta,* published in 1894, where to describe a stream of consciousness he speaks of Aminta's "dotting" her thoughts.
3. For these and similar objections by contemporaries cf., besides the authors themselves, J. A. Hammerton, *George Meredith, His Life and Art in Anecdote and Criticism.*
4. "The treasure of verse is where thought embraces feeling, as the man the woman. Then you have joined the highest in mind with the deepest in nature. That is why Poetry is above philosophy: it is the voice of essential man before the Gods." (Quoted by R. E. Gordon George, "Unpublished Letters of George Meredith," and dated by him as of 1887).
5. In chapter sixteen of *One of Our Conquerors* he speaks of it as being not a "remote Externe, who plays the human figures," but something "beside us, within us, our breath, if we will."
6. Cf. Robert E. Sencourt (R. E. Gordon George), *The Life of George Meredith,* 67. Lady Butcher paraphrases from a conversation in which Meredith stressed the fact that "the body should be dominated and disciplined, not starved and denied." (*Memories of George Meredith,* 110-111).
7. Purcell Barrett and the Earl of Fleetwood are examples of spiritual loneliness and consequent warping of personality. G. K. Chesterton contrasts Meredith and Hardy—"The argument of Meredith is that our little lives always stagnate into hypocrisy or morbidity, unless the general wave of the world continually refreshes and recreates us." ("The Moral Philosophy of Meredith").

8. Cf. Hammerton, *op. cit.,* 81.
9. *Letters of George Meredith,* 333 and *passim.*
10. Meredith used the term *tragic comedian* to mean a person at one and the same time tragic and comic. In this study I have employed the traditional *tragicomic,* not in the loose sense to describe a narrative at times tragic at others comic, but to characterize tragic comedians and their experiences.
11. For discussion of Meredith's interest in Goethe cf. John Lees, "George Meredith's Literary Relations with Germany," and Guy B. Petter, *George Meredith and His German Critics.*
12. The letter to Jessopp is wrongly dated in *Letters.* Both it and the letter of June 18, 1874, quoted in chapter six, are reproduced with minor inaccuracies. For the MS. reading of both I am indebted to Miss Barbara D. Simison, of the Yale University Library. For uniformity with *Letters* I have transcribed *&* as *and.*
13. Cf. A. H. Able, *George Meredith and Thomas Love Peacock: A Study in Literary Influence.*
14. For discussions of Meredith's work as a journalist cf. S. M. Ellis, *George Meredith: His Life and Friends in Relation to His Work,* 198 and *passim,* and Siegfried Sassoon, *Meredith,* 66.
15. In chapter thirty of *One of Our Conquerors* Meredith generalizes upon the irrational demands made on women by late-Victorian civilization:

    > Thus was she [Nesta], too, being put into her woman's harness of the bit and the blinkers, and taught to know herself for the weak thing, the gentle parasite, which the fiction of our civilization expects her, caressingly and contemptuously, to become in the active, while it is exacted of her—O Comedy of Clowns!—that in the passive she be a rock-fortress impregnable, not to speak of magically encircled.

    Needless to say, Nesta atypically casts the harness aside.
16. Examples early and late include: "We are still fighting against the Puritan element, in literature as elsewhere" (*Sandra Belloni,* chapter eight); "It's [Christian gentleman] the cant of a detestable school . . . The professors mainly profess to be 'a comfort to young women' . . . There's no absolute harm in them, only that they're a

sentimental compromise. I deny their honesty; and if it's flatly proved, I deny their intelligence" (*Sandra Belloni,* chapter twenty-eight; though in dialogue, the views are the author's); "Professional Puritans, born conservatives, malicious tattlers . . ." (*Lord Ormont,* chapter fifteen). To Maxse the novelist wrote (in 1862, according to *Letters*), "What you say about Christianity arresting sensualism, is very well: but the Essenian parentage of Christianity was simply asceticism. Hitherto human nature has marched through the conflict of extremes. With the general growth of reason, it will be possible to choose a path mid-way. Paganism no doubt deserved the ascetic reproof; but Christianity failed to supply much that it destroyed." (*Letters,* 67).

17. For the most thorough discussion of Richter's influence on the *Essay* cf. E. V. Brewer, "The Influence of Jean Paul Richter on George Meredith's Conception of the Comic."
18. The extent to which Meredith's works, including *Evan Harrington,* are autobiographic is discussed by S. M. Ellis, *op. cit.* Ellis' generalizations have sometimes been qualified by Sassoon and others.
19. In "Sir Willoughby's Pattern" and "The Egoist and the Willow Pattern," R. D. Mayo shows that the willow-pattern story was well known and used by Meredith's friend F. C. Burnand in "A Tale of Old China," which ran from April 19 to July 3, 1875, as a "German Reed entertainment at St. George's Hall."
20. He also eliminated the death at her child's grave of Kiomi, the victim of Heriot's seduction, and Heriot's own death on an Indian battlefield. That he should originally write such a sentimental ending for Kiomi suggests his immersion in the sentiment of the age; that he rejected it reveals the reassertion of brain.
21. For information on the composition of each novel cf., besides the special studies listed in the bibliography, *Letters* and M. Buxton Forman, *A Bibliography of George Meredith...* Revisions of the novels are indicated also in the Memorial edition of *The Works of George Meredith,* volume twenty-seven.
22. Cf. *supra,* note 12.
23. For the development of *Rhoda Fleming* from a "plain story" to a complex novel, cf. C. J. Hill, "George Mere-

dith's 'Plain Story'." Professor Hill also shows the influence upon Meredith of *Clarissa Harlowe, The Heart of Midlothian,* and *Adam Bede.*

24. Guy B. Petter, *op. cit.,* summarizes German discussions of the betrayal. There are comments also in several of the critical works in English.
25. " 'Diana of the Crossways' keeps me still on her sad last way to wedlock. I could have killed her merrily, with my compliments to the public; and that was my intention. But the marrying of her, sets me traversing feminine labyrinths, and you know that the why of it never can be accounted for." (To Mrs. Leslie Stephen, May 19, 1884, *Letters,* 357). At what time in the process of composing he changed his intention is not clear. Certainly there are touches long before the betrayal which are in harmony only with a happy ending, and they do not appear to be later insertions. While completing *Diana* Meredith was weighed down by the serious and, as it proved, fatal illness of Mrs. Meredith. His physical and nervous fatigue may have helped to account for the inadequate presentation of his heroine's personality; it could hardly explain the anticlimactic structure of the novel.
26. In "The Artistic Unity of 'Richard Feverel': Chapter XXXIII," W. E. Buckler demonstrates that Sir Austin's motives prevent the working of any system. Cf. also W. R. Mueller, "Theological Dualism and the 'System' in *Richard Feverel.*"
27. Cf. *supra,* note 10.
28. For discussion of Meredith's knowledge of Helene von Racowitza's (*née* Dönniges) *Meine Beziehungen zu Ferdinand Lassalle,* which appeared in 1879, and of other documents pertaining to the actual historical incidents, cf. John Lees, "George Meredith's Literary Relations with Germany," and H. W. Hewett-Thayer, "Ferdinand Lassalle in the Novels of Spielhagen and Meredith." The latter is the more accurate and the more reliable bibliographically.

Important Dates in Meredith's Life

February 12, 1828 Birth

August, 1842–1844 Schooling at Neuwied

July 7, 1849 Publication of "Chillianwallah," his first printed poem

August 9, 1849 Marriage to Mary Nicolls

June, 1853 Birth of Arthur Meredith

1855 Publication of *The Shaving of Shagpat*

1860–1868 Writing for *The Ipswich Journal*

1860–1895 Reading for Chapman and Hall

October, 1861 Death of Mary N. Meredith, after estrangement since 1858

September 20, 1864 Marriage to Marie Vulliamy

Summer, 1866 Corresponding on the Italian War for *The Morning Post*

September 17, 1885 Death of Marie V. Meredith

May 18, 1909 Death of George Meredith

Chronology of Works

(Selected list. For complete chronology of poems cf. M. B. Forman, *A Bibliography . . .*)

1851 *Love in the Valley* (rewritten version 1878)
1855 *The Shaving of Shagpat*
1857 *Farina*
1859 *The Ordeal of Richard Feverel* (revised version 1875)
1860 *Evan Harrington*
1862 *Modern Love*
1864 *Emilia in England* (*Sandra Belloni*)
1865 *Rhoda Fleming*
1867 *Vittoria*
1871 *The Adventures of Harry Richmond*
1875 *Beauchamp's Career*
1877 *The House on the Beach*
1877 *The Case of General Ople and Lady Camper*
1877 *An Essay on Comedy and the Uses of the Comic Spirit*
1879 *The Tale of Chloe*
1879 *The Egoist*
1880 *The Tragic Comedians*
1885 *Diana of the Crossways*
1891 *One of Our Conquerors*
1894 *Lord Ormont and His Aminta*
1895 *The Amazing Marriage*
1910 *Celt and Saxon* (unfinished)

Bibliography

Meredith's Literary Works and Letters

The Works of George Meredith, Scribners Memorial Edition, 29 vols. New York: 1909-1912 (includes letters ed. by W. M. Meredith)

Letters from George Meredith to Edward Clodd and Clement K. Shorter. Privately printed: 1913

Letters from George Meredith to Richard Henry Horne. Privately printed: 1919

Letters from George Meredith to Algernon Charles Swinburne and Theodore Watts-Dunton. Privately printed: 1922

The Letters of George Meredith to Alice Meynell. London: 1923

Letters of George Meredith to Various Correspondents. Privately printed: 1924

George, R. E. "Unpublished Letters of George Meredith," *The Nineteenth Century and After,* CIII (1928), 149-162

Bibliographical Studies

Forman, M. Buxton. *A Bibliography of the Writings in Prose and Verse of George Meredith.* Edinburgh: 1922

Forman, M. Buxton. *Meredithiana, Being a Supplement to the Bibliography of Meredith...* Edinburgh: 1924 (lists reviews and other references to Meredith)

Coolidge, Bertha. *A Catalogue of the Altschul Collection of George Meredith in the Yale University Library.* Privately printed: 1931

Selected Studies, Biographical and Critical

Photiadès, Constantin. *George Meredith, sa vie—son imagination—son art —sa doctrine.* Paris: 1910

Butcher, Alice M. (Lady). *Memories of George Meredith.* New York: 1919

Ellis, S. M. *George Meredith, His Life and Friends in Relation to His Work.* New York: 1920

Galland, René. *George Meredith; les cinquante premières années (1828-1878).* Paris: 1923

Gretton, Mary S. *The Writings and Life of George Meredith.* Cambridge: 1926

George (Sencourt), R. E. *The Life of George Meredith.* New York: 1929

Zipf, G. K. "New Facts in the Early Life of George Meredith," *Harvard Studies and Notes in Philol. and Lit.,* XX (1938), 131-145

Sassoon, Siegfried. *Meredith.* New York: 1948

Selected Studies, Mainly Critical

Monkhouse, Allan. "Mr. Meredith's Novels," *Books and Plays.* Philadelphia: 1894

Oliphant, James. "George Meredith," *Victorian Novelists.* London: 1899

Le Gallienne, Richard. *George Meredith, Some Characteristics.* New York: 1900

Brownell, Wm. C. "George Meredith," *Victorian Prose Masters.* New York: 1915 (essay on Meredith in 1901)

Legouis, Émile. "L'Égoiste de George Meredith," *Revue germanique,* I (1905), 403-430

More, P. E. "The Novels of George Meredith," *Shelburne Essays,* Second Series. New York: 1905

Trevelyan, G. M. *The Poetry and Philosophy of George Meredith.* New York: 1906

Bailey, E. J. *The Novels of George Meredith: A Study.* New York: 1907

Curle, Richard. *Aspects of George Meredith.* New York: 1908

Chesterton, G. K. "The Moral Philosophy of Meredith," *Contemporary Review,* XCVI (1909), 23-28

McKechnie, James. *Meredith's Allegory, The Shaving of Shagpat, Interpreted.* London: 1910

Beach, J. W. *The Comic Spirit in George Meredith: An Interpretation.* New York: 1911

Hammerton, J. A. *George Meredith, His Life and Art in Anecdote and Criticism.* Edinburgh: 1911 (summarizes at length earlier criticisms, including many not listed here)

Lees, John. "George Meredith's Literary Relations with Germany," *Modern Lang. Review,* XII (1917), 428-437

Sherman, S. P. "The Humanism of George Meredith," *On Contemporary Literature.* New York: 1917

Dimond, Charles. "Music in the Novels of George Meredith," *The Nineteenth Cent. and After,* LXXXVII (1920), 845-850

Strong, Archibald. "Nature in Wordsworth and Meredith," *Three Studies in Shelley.* London: 1921

Galland, René. *George Meredith and British Criticism (1851-1909).* Paris: 1923

Wolff, Lucien. *George Meredith, poète et romancier; introduction à son oeuvre.* Paris: 1924

Priestley, J. B. *George Meredith.* London: 1926

Turquet-Milnes, Gladys. "Meredith and the Cosmic Spirit," *From Pascal to Proust.* New York: 1926

Brewer, E. V. "The Influence of Jean Paul Richter on George Meredith's Conception of the Comic," *Journal of Engl. and Germ. Philol.,* XXIX (1930), 243-256

Roberts, W. W. "Music in Meredith," *Music and Letters,* XIII (1932), 255-263

Able, A. H., III. *George Meredith and Thomas Love Peacock: A Study in Literary Influence.* Philadelphia: 1933

Lowes, J. L. "An Unacknowledged Imagist," *Essays in Appreciation.* New York: 1936

Mainland, W. F. "A German Source for *The Shaving of Shagpat*?" *Modern Lang. Review,* XXXI (1936), 408-410

Baker, E. A. *The History of the English Novel,* Vol. VIII, Chapters 7-9. London: 1937

Woods, Alice. *George Meredith as Champion of Women and of Progressive Education.* Oxford: 1937

Robinson, E. A. "Meredith's Literary Theory and Science: Realism vs. the Comic Spirit," *PMLA,* LIII (1938), 857-868

Petter, G. B. *George Meredith and His German Critics.* London: 1939

Mayo, R. D. "Sir Willoughby's Pattern," *Notes and Queries,* CLXXXIII (1942), 362-363

Mayo, R. D. "*The Egoist* and the Willow Pattern," *Engl. Lit. Hist.,* IX (1942), 71-78

Hewett-Thayer, H. W. "Ferdinand Lassalle in the Novels of Spielhagen and Meredith," *Germanic Review,* XIX (1944), 186-196

Ekeberg, Gladys. "*The Ordeal of Richard Feverel* as Tragedy," *College English,* VII (1946), 387-393

Going, W. T. "A Note on 'My Lady' of *Modern Love*," *Modern Lang. Quarterly,* VII (1946), 311-314

Hudson, R. B. "The Meaning of Egoism in George Meredith's *The Egoist*," *The Trollopian,* III (1948), 163-176

Gettmann, R. A. "Meredith as Publisher's Reader," *Journal of Engl. and Germ. Philol.,* XLVIII (1949), 45-56

Gettmann, R. A. "Serialization and *Evan Harrington*," *PMLA,* LXIV (1949), 963-975

Eaker, J. G. "Meredith's Human Comedy," *Nineteenth Century Fiction,* V (1951), 253-272

Mueller, W. R. "Theological Dualism and the 'System' in *Richard Feverel*," *Engl. Lit. Hist.,* XVIII (1951), 138-154

Hill, C. J. "George Meredith's 'Plain Story'," *Nineteenth Century Fiction,* VII (1952), 90-102

Buckler, W. E. "The Artistic Unity of 'Richard Feverel': Chapter XXXIII," *Nineteenth Century Fiction,* VII (1952), 119-123

Index of Meredith's Works